'LOVED IT! This is one of those books you'll be high-lighting and dog-earring for months. You'll come back to it. It's a full body of work but easy to imple-ment in chunks. Laetitia's superpower is blending practical and actionable strategy with a rock-solid mindset. If you have a business or even dream of having one, do yourself a favour and read this book.'

KATIE ROSE, Author of *Mindful Living*

'A must-read book for thriving in business without burning out. *Light It* offers a practical and spiritual take on entrepreneurship. Laetitia leads the way with an innovative and intuitive approach to business without sacrificing yourself. Her signature LIGHT framework will guide you in (re)designing your busi-ness in true alignment.'

TINA TOWER, Author of *Million Dollar Micro Business* and *One Life*

'*Light It* is a must read for anyone who's come crash-ing down off the "you can have it all" treadmill to find themselves living a burnt out, less fulfilling ver-sion of the life they imagined. Laetitia's signature LIGHT framework pairs her business savvy and well-ness-first approach with actionable strategies and a refreshing "tell it like it is" approach to uncover the unique beauty in running a soul-aligned business. If you're looking for a soft, nourishing kick in the butt, *Light It* offers a new roadmap to success that priori-tises both productivity and self-care and lets you live a life you love.'

ELISE STRACHAN, Author of *Sweet! Celebrations*

'A whirlwind of strategy, pragmatism and rituals. Laetitia Andrac is a much-needed voice to define a new paradigm in leadership and entrepreneurship. If you are stuck and looking for the next step, read this book and connect with your light again.'

EMILYA COLLIVER, Author of *The Art Project* and Founder of Art Pharmacy

'*Light It* was exactly what I needed to read. With raw vulnerability and insight, Laetitia Andrac offers practical advice about how to grow your business, how to say no to burn out and trust that your own intuition will guide you ... If you're feeling burnout or need motivation, the wisdom in this book and the inspiring stories will make you see your potential from the inside out. Be prepared to shine and take action!'

MOLLY BENJAMIN, Author of *Girls Wanna Have Funds* and Founder of Ladies Finance Club

'Laetitia provides a roadmap to break the business-building burnout mould. Her LIGHT framework is the perfect blend of business strategy, intuition and a holistic approach to shaping the work you want to do in alignment with the life you want to live. Do yourself a favour and dive in with an open mind and heart.'

PENNY LOCASO, Author of *Hacking Happiness: How to Intentionally Adapt and Shape the Future You Want*

'I've flirted with burnout too many times now to be complacent or think, "I know this already." Self-empowerment is not a one-and-done thing; we have to be (gently) vigilant to our patterns if we want our businesses to make a big difference in the world. Laetitia's book has helped me understand the connection between my heart, body and mind. Even if you're sceptical about your own intuition or feel "too busy" to slow down, you'll find simple and doable steps to do business differently and sustainably so you can feel more joy and connection again.'

DENISE DUFFIELD-THOMAS, Founder of Money Bootcamp, and Author of *Chill and Prosper*

'This book is a guide, and a teaching that will serve all who find themselves approaching or experiencing burnout. Laetitia shares her story of recovery through reconnecting with fundamental principles. She makes ancient spiritual wisdom and intuition accessible for busy modern-day entrepreneurs. Everyone should read this at the beginning of their career to connect with their intuition and achieve better health and harmony.'

JANE HARDWICKE COLLINGS, Founder of the School of Shamanic Womancraft and Author of *Ten Moons: The Inner Journey of Pregnancy*

'This is a brilliant, profound, raw and timely read. If you're an entrepreneur who is feeling disconnected, exhausted and on the brink of burnout, this book offers hope and a practical framework to guide you. Laetitia is helping us all to realise that building a successful business goes hand in hand with following your intuition. This book is a must read for anyone considering the path of entrepreneurship or well on their way to leading a fast-growing business.'

SHEREE RUBINSTEIN, Founder of One Roof

'Laetitia is the real deal when it comes to doing business with purpose and passion; head and heart. Her lessons and learnings are an opportunity to pause, reset and breathe; to tap into your inner wisdom and smile at any and every part of your entrepreneurial journey. If you want to do business better, you need to do it in the right way for you—that's what this book will help you achieve.'

KELLY IRVING, Book Coach, Editor and Founder of The Expert Author Community

'Fascinating life lessons from a woman brave enough to question why we do business the way we do.'

ADAM SPENCER, Speaker, Comedian, Maths Geek and Author of *Maths 101*

LIGHT IT

LIGHT IT

How to Trust Your Intuition and
Build a Thriving Business

Laetitia Andrac

Published by Grammar Factory Publishing,
an imprint of MacMillan Company Limited.

Grammar Factory Publishing
MacMillan Company Limited
25 Telegram Mews, 39th Floor, Suite 3906
Toronto, Ontario, Canada
M5V 3Z1

www.grammarfactory.com

Andrac, Laetitia, 1984–
Light It: How to Trust Your Intuition and
Build a Thriving Business / Laetitia Andrac.

Paperback ISBN 978-1-998756-35-3
Hardcover ISBN 978-1-998756-37-7
eBook ISBN 978-1-998756-36-0

1. BUS025000 BUSINESS & ECONOMICS / Entrepreneurship.
2. BUS071000 BUSINESS & ECONOMICS/Leadership. 3. BUS046000
BUSINESS & ECONOMICS / Motivational.

Production Credits

Cover design by Designerbility
Interior layout design by Setareh Ashrafologhalai
Book production and editorial services by Grammar Factory Publishing

Grammar Factory's Carbon Neutral Publishing Commitment
Grammar Factory Publishing is proud to be neutralizing the carbon
footprint of all printed copies of its authors' books printed by or ordered
directly through Grammar Factory or its affiliated companies through
the purchase of Gold Standard-Certified International Offsets.

*To those who are ready to step into
their light to lead themselves and
their business with sacredness.*

*To those who have come before me,
I hope I am honouring your teachings.*

*To Johan, my husband, my
soul mate, my best friend.*

*To my two daughters, Zoe and Lou. You
have taught me to connect to my intuition
more than I ever thought possible.*

*I respectfully acknowledge the First Nations
people of Country throughout Australia and
pay my respects to Elders past and present.*

*I acknowledge the cultural and spiritual
connection that Aboriginal and Torres Strait
Islander peoples have with the land and sea.*

*May we learn from their ancestral
ways to walk gently on Country and
live more harmoniously with ourselves,
each other and the natural world.*

CONTENTS

INTRODUCTION

I T WAS 2014. I was a Strategy Consultant in France at the top of my game. Picture the lifestyle that comes from living in Paris and working hard. Good food, good wine and good company. I was wearing designer clothes and carrying handbags from Prada, Chanel and Marc Jacobs. My high-heeled shoes were from Louboutin. The world's most renowned red sole was giving me the confidence I needed to keep going. As I write this, you may be watching *Emily in Paris*, the popular Netflix original series. Well, I was Emily, but a French Emily. I was thirty; nothing could stop me. I was a six-figure earner at the top of my game. I loved my career, but it was a lot—a lot of work and sacrifice. I would eat out in high-end restaurants and go to the opera in Palais Garnier or Opéra Bastille every month. As part of my job benefits, I was given unlimited access to Centre Pompidou, Le Louvre and Musée d'Orsay. I loved immersing myself in the beauty of the museums. I was travelling Europe, working around the clock on three major projects, leading a team and preparing for a wedding at the same time. I was the 'career woman' who was in the taxi at 10 pm heading home from work and back in the taxi again at 6 am returning to the office. At the same time as writing proposals and thought leadership papers, I was mentoring new leaders and serving different clients in different places. It really was all about the hustle. If you allow me to name drop, I even met Mike Bloomberg (one of our clients) in Berlin while working on a Bloomberg Philanthropies project. The goal of the project was to help mayors of twenty-one cities in Europe to develop creative solutions to their most pressing social and economic issues, and to meet the challenges of tomorrow in areas from education to public safety.

While I loved what I was doing—the projects I was working on and the opportunities I had—I was disconnected and drained. I wasn't present, and it felt like life was rushing past me. I wasn't even getting daily sunlight, let alone connecting to the seasons of life. I was barely meeting my own basic human needs, so you can imagine I wasn't doing any form of self-care. Most of the time, I would look outside myself for confirmation that I was doing great. I was identified as an emerging leader and ranked in the top ten per cent of my peers. I was even selected to represent successful female leaders with Deloitte's CEO at the time, Barry Salzburg. I was interviewed on a documentary for French TV to showcase what a successful woman in leadership looked like. And I was recognised as a leader in innovation as Deloitte's point of contact with Doblin (a premium boutique innovation consultant in the US that we acquired). I had a promising future working in strategy for our practice, with a promotion to an even higher role in the leadership team on the horizon.

But as I see it, life is not black or white; there is always an in-between. Maybe as you read this, you say regularly:

'I love my career, but…' *or*
'I love my business, but…'

When we aren't aligned with our true selves and passion in life, there is always a 'but'. Without self-care, it's easy to get lost on life's journey and forget about our basic needs, which are the foundation of our success. Because I wasn't listening to my body, I never gave myself a chance to recharge. Just like a battery, we need recharging too. Before I could get trapped in this 'hustle' mentality, I made space to reconnect with my intuition. I grew up in a family deeply connected with the seasons, the moon cycle and energy. My father, aunty and grandparents would teach me about intuition, energy healing and connection with the cycles of nature. We would go on hikes, harvest wild mushrooms in the deep forests and go for naked swims in the open sea.

I remember my grandma looking at the moon phases and the season, then telling me: 'We need to plant green beans today!' or 'It is time to harvest the potatoes today!' It was all very sacred. I was taught that Earth's natural rhythms influenced everything we did in our lives. But when I entered one of the best business schools in the world, I was ashamed of that past, of my humble and modest family. I was catapulted into an alien world that didn't appreciate me or my wonderful upbringing. I know now that my roots, my ancestral lineage, are the richest part of my identity. At the time, being that version of me—the true me—didn't align with my peers. So, I slowly disconnected from this inner knowing, the ancestral knowing, this communion with the Earth, the moon, the seasons, nature and my intuition. I was following someone else's advice and vision of success. I was outsourcing my intuition! After graduating from one of the top 10 business schools in the world, I entered one of the best consulting firms in Europe—divorcing myself even farther from my roots. As I write these words, tears are rolling down my cheeks. I slowly disconnected from myself to the point I no longer noticed the beautiful seasons of the world and my life. I was utterly disembodied from what I loved to do when I was young, from meditating and dancing to singing and connecting with nature. There were many days that I don't even recall going outside! Does this sound familiar?

That was when it all came crashing down. I'm a hyperactive person, so I don't get tired often. I have two young girls who don't sleep a lot, and when tiredness comes to me, it doesn't affect me like most people. So, when I say I'm tired, something is definitely wrong! It was mid-June in 2014 when I woke up, turned to my partner and said, 'I'm exhausted.'

I physically couldn't move that day. I was lying in bed with no energy, drive or willingness to do anything. This was the moment I realised I needed to see a doctor. I booked my appointment that same day and took my first day off in years. There were days I would go to the office so sick that I'd be vomiting and have to hide the fact that I was unwell. This was the environment I worked in. If you were sick, your ego would take over and tell you, 'Keep going; you can't have a day off. If you have a day off, someone else might take the next best opportunity.'

So, I sat in the doctor's office while she read a series of questions. Then, she said it. 'You are experiencing burnout.' Her words hit me hard. I burst into tears. At that time, I thought burnout happened to fragile people. I was *not* a fragile person. I was a Strategic Manager at one of the top firms in Paris. People like me (at the time) didn't burn out. Or so I thought.

Of course, now I know burnout is anything but a sign of weakness. Listening to your body and recognising burnout is a life-saving skill. Learning to listen to your body *before* burning out is the best skill of all, but more on that later.

I felt deep shame when that diagnosis came out of the doctor's mouth and into my ears. Growing up in the French countryside, I was raised with ancestral spiritual gifts and a deep connection to the land. I learned meditation as young as five years old. I travelled and lived in countries like Brazil, Senegal and India (to name a few). In my early twenties, I learned so much about ancient spiritual wisdom. I used the tools of that wisdom and experienced their powers in trance meditation. But somewhere along the line, I lost all of this. I was not active and not eating nourishing food; I was drinking, partying and living a crazy lifestyle. This was not how I was raised.

I was extracting myself from where I came from. While I thought I was doing what was best for me and my career, I had utterly lost track of my spiritual rituals. I had lost connection with myself and my intuition. When I burned out, it was my body's way of saying, 'This is enough. You must stop and reconnect with your light, your intuition and yourself.'

We are all too busy being busy, thinking we are doing our best when, in fact, the opposite is true.

This is how the journey to where I am (now) all started. This is the story that changed everything for me. We all have one of those. Maybe you are going through it right now. If you are, then know you are not alone, and I can promise you there is a light at the end of the tunnel. But first, you have to commit to the journey and, most importantly, trust in yourself.

THERE IS TIME TO CHANGE!

If burning out is what it takes to succeed in strategy consulting, I decided it wasn't for me. Within a few months of burning out, I made a big shift. After my wedding, my partner and I decided to try something new. For the first time in a long time, I connected to my intuition; Australia was calling me. Without ever visiting Australia, I knew it would be the perfect place to reconnect with my intuition, to heal myself, others and the land. So we headed to Australia. We arrived on 15 October 2014; I didn't have a job or plan, but I already knew I was home. I was learning to trust myself again.

I took a career break and held space for myself during this time. I did yoga and reconnected with nature (especially on Bondi Beach in summer). I took many courses to learn about shamanic practices, deepened my ayurvedic knowledge, and practised meditation and yoga nidra. It didn't make sense then, but I followed my intuition. The transformation happened as I leaned in and embraced the void left by not working in a nine to five job. Not everyone can have this luxury, but I enjoyed it for six months. Then, for visa reasons, I started looking for a new role. In April 2015, I started working at a corporate job that would eventually lead me into my full-time entrepreneur career.

When I opted for this nine-to-five role, I was very transparent with my boss who hired me. I shared my experience with burnout, and I shared openly about my gifts. My intuitive side was always kept secret at work until I moved to Australia. I chose this corporate job because I knew it would give me the space, time and energy to succeed without sending me back into burnout.

While working in my corporate role, I began the search for my true calling. I never forced it; I just tried and trusted. As a side hustle, I experimented with three businesses (you'll read about it later) before creating Essential Shift, my current consulting company. I failed, learned and grew during this process, but I did things differently this time. I made sure to reconnect to myself and my intuition along the way.

Most of all, I connected to my vision. Although it took trial and error to find my true calling, the vision was clear. I wanted to impact millions of women across the globe. I wanted to help them find alignment, lead authentically, and trust their intuition before they reach burnout, as I experienced, or help them heal. I knew I had to blend my ancient wisdom teachings with my business sense. I knew I had to create something unique that didn't put me in a box but allowed me to stand on it and shout from the rooftops. I created something just like this book—not just a business book, spiritual book, or self-development book—but something unique that spoke directly to women. This is me, honouring being different.

Everything amplified and accelerated in 2021 when a friend, who I used to work with in strategy consulting, passed away suddenly from cancer. This book came to me as a mission to share more about looking after yourself as a leader, a Sacred CEO, before it is too late.

Here I am! Presenting these teachings to you! So, hi! I am Laetitia Andrac, an energetics and strategy business mentor (or, as my clients call me, a 'business doula'). After I burned out in 2014, I committed to helping other entrepreneurs prevent burnout and connect more with their true selves. I believe I have created a truly unique experience for my clients, blending my journey through the spiritual world of energetics with the world of corporate leadership.

I started Essential Shift in 2021. Since then, I have been nominated for the Australian Small Business Champion Award (2023), written a monthly column in a renowned holistic life magazine, and impacted thousands of entrepreneurs across the globe.

This business has grown over half a million dollars in less than two years, with lots of freedom and flexibility. I can pick up my girls from school at 3 pm, spend holidays in France, take long lunches and go on retreats frequently. But it isn't just about having a flexible life. My business fills my soul; I see a range of business owners and professionals heal and build their dream businesses because of it. I've even had clients grow their revenue to eight figures in eighteen months. I am making ancient spiritual wisdom and intuition accessible to busy modern-day entrepreneurs. And it's bringing them amazing success. Let's make it accessible for you too!

Why I wrote this book

Picture this. It's 9 pm, and you're still working on your never-ending to-do list at your office desk. Even when you tick one thing off, another thing gets added. You've missed dinner with your partner again. You started this business so you could be with your family and travel more, but here you are. You're sitting at your desk, working more than you did in your nine to five. Don't worry if this sounds like you; you are not alone.

In this new world of digital connection and always being on the go, we can often become disconnected and unaligned with our vision, purpose and life calling.

This leads to increased stress levels and disconnection, especially for entrepreneurs, who often prioritise being busy, working and 'hustling' over looking after their health and well-being.

At the time of this book's publication, we're witnessing a movement called the Great Resignation, amplified by the COVID-19 pandemic. More people are looking for ways to find meaning again, to grow a business without burning out—a business that allows more time for family, travel and joy.

I know you want this too, but maybe you feel you are in too deep. How do you take more off your to-do list? How do you create more income without more work?

The problem isn't about looking to people who have 'done it before'. It is not learning more about business models or how to build a funnel. It is about trusting yourself.

It is about learning more about using your intuition in business and looking for the answers within you, not outside of you. It is time to stop outsourcing your intuition, your most unique asset in business.

So many books on the market are designed to help you 'get rich quick' on strategies that work to the detriment of your health and intuition. Building a sustainable business for yourself, your team and the planet shouldn't come at the cost of these things.

I also see many books that teach about manifestation, energetics or spirituality in a way that lacks grounding. It is hard for someone to succeed using unfamiliar practices, let alone get the 'dream life' outcome if they lack the basic understanding.

So, I wrote this book to help you blend your strategic business brain with your intuition and blend the two in a grounded way. This book is about combining the business, the energetics and the intuition of your soul into one being.

That is my purpose. This is what led me to write this book. Intuition in business comes through experimenting, so this book is broken into two parts.

Part One explores the reality of burnout and why your hustle-oriented lifestyle may not work for your business. You will learn how to connect with your intuition and why it will help you to succeed in business. In a nutshell, we unpack why leveraging intuition and strategy are both important.

Part Two breaks down the LIGHT framework into bite-sized pieces to help you develop a roadmap of daily connection with your intuition and business.

You'll learn the power of Leaning in, Illuminating, Gathering, Honouring and Transforming to unleash a new way of running your business. LIGHT is the key to creating a life by design.

What is LIGHT? It is intuition, alignment and connection with our inner knowing. LIGHT is how we become our own beacon, our own lighthouse. By discovering our illuminated path to success, we can lead others in connecting with their authority, their authentic selves and their light. One of my beautiful Aboriginal guides, Minmia, shares in her book, *Under the Quandong Tree*, 'All around light is darkness. With lots and lots of candles, there is light to see our way. If we go blowing out the candles, all we're left with is darkness. Can we stop ourselves from putting out the lights?'

Remember, connecting with intuition is a life-long process. This is your journey. Not anyone else's. While you might find yourself looking at what others are doing, the point of this book is to start finding the answers to create a business that works for you, not the other way around. The journey is a marathon, not a sprint. Your business isn't going anywhere. Connecting with your intuition means you do things your way. And if you are saying to yourself: 'I am not intuitive,' let me share a truthbomb now with you: We are all intuitive beings! By the end of this book, you will have all the tools you need to always look within for answers and trust yourself 100 per cent when making any decision.

Although it might sound counterintuitive, my goal for this book is to make my work redundant! If you apply this LIGHT framework and connect to the teachings herein, you won't need me to help you grow your business or connect with your rituals. When you reclaim your light, you need less coaching, mentoring and leadership help. You step into your power as a leader. Imagine your LIGHT as a source of reflection for a disco ball—without it, it can't shine. Your business is just like that disco ball, and your intuition is light. Are you ready to be the leader of your business?

How to get the most from your journey

Whenever I mention that I blend energetics and business, people are curious. 'What does that look like?' they often ask. But it comes down to intuition for those who aren't so spiritual. You don't have to be 'super spiritual' to get the most from this book. So, what is intuition?

You know the saying 'trust your gut'? Well, that gut feeling you sometimes get is intuition. When you search for intuition in the dictionary, you get this simple explanation: 'The ability to understand something immediately, without the need for conscious reasoning.'

When you connect with your intuition, it isn't attached to any emotion, but you know it is right. You don't feel scared, stressed or anxious; you just have this feeling of peace and understanding.

Have you ever heard someone in business say, 'I don't know why I did it; I just did'? This is a great example of intuition. Some might even liken the feeling of intuition to leading with their heart instead of their head. When you lead with your heart, magical things happen.

We must step away from this anxiety, stress and hustle mentality in business. Reclaim your intuition and start being a leader for yourself before others. When you do, you will create true magic in your business.

If you don't lead from this place of groundedness and connection, your business will suffer from a lack of adaptability. Furthermore, if you lack agility in your business, it's likely because you are not following your heart. When entrepreneurs have more time to connect with their intuition, they can make more informed and insightful decisions that can positively impact their business. If you are a CEO, Director or team leader in any capacity, guiding your team with intuition at the heart is even more important. It is a powerful and light way forward. Building agility and adaptability into your business is essential as technology transforms how entrepreneurs work. For example, AI (artificial intelligence) liberates entrepreneurs by automating repetitive tasks and allowing them to focus on higher-level work requiring more intuition and creativity.

In a world of ever-growing artificial intelligence, our natural, native intelligence, instincts, intuition, empathy and ever-unfolding life experience will become more important as technology obscures their value. However, it is this instinct and intuition that makes us human. As long as we embrace our intuition, AI will never fully replace us.

I often compare this journey of intuition in business to growing a garden. You plant the seeds, but that is only the first part of the work. You must water these seeds and watch them grow. There might be times when you need to give the garden more love, and the garden creates different flowers during different seasons. With any garden, you must give it time and trust the process. This is what you must do when you run a business backed by your intuition.

To help you get the most from this book and the journey you will embark on, I have put together a few tips.

Step 1: Start with an open mind, an open heart and an open will

Start this journey with an open mind, an open heart and an open will to change how you've been running your business and step into your leadership as a business owner. It is time for deep listening. You get stuck in your old stories if you don't listen deeply. You know what they say; nothing changes if nothing changes. It is time to never say never and connect with a new way of doing things. This will help you to harness your full potential. Yes, your ego will get in the way at some point as you read this book. Honour that and move forward. If you read this book half-heartedly, your garden won't grow. So ask yourself, are you open to learning a new way of business?

Step 2: Do the work

You will need a journal and a pen for this book. You can even have a dedicated journal or notebook for each exercise. Go through and do the exercises one by one. Make sure you trust the process of each exercise; they all serve the purpose of helping you connect with your intuition. This way, you can stop the hustle and start building a business that works for you.

Step 3: Come back when you need to

You can read this book cover to cover but return to the areas you need to if you get lost. You might be eager to reach the end goal of your transformation, but you must go through the journey first. Nothing happens overnight, so enjoy this new experience and know the work continues once you are done. It's up to you to decide what areas of your business (or life) you will work on in the future, but keep this book handy to guide you if you lose your way.

REMEMBER: this journey (guided by the book) allows you to do things differently. To stop the hustle. To stop the traditional way of working so you can build the lifestyle you envisioned when the idea of your business was just a seed.

With burnout and hustle culture becoming more prevalent (and toxic) than ever, it is time for something different.

It is time to start having dinner with your family; it is time to get off that business hamster wheel and start connecting with yourself again.

This book will give you the tools to do that. Stop working. Start living.

PART 1

FROM DISCONNECTION TO RECONNECTION

Get ready, because in part I we will be talking about:

- The risk of staying disconnected from your business, and

- How intuition can help fuel your business confidence.

THE REALITY OF BEING DISCONNECTED

A STORY OF DISCONNECTION THAT LED TO WORSE THAN BURNOUT

Mariah is a full-time business owner. After quitting her corporate job in 2020, she was set on the digital nomad, entrepreneur life. What also happened in 2020? As we know, COVID-19 set the world on fire. With a fresh business, Mariah spent a lot of this time working.

She loved it. Even when we weren't in lockdown, Mariah was always in her hustle energy. While juggling her side hustle and a full-time corporate job, she also went to the gym five days a week. She would get up at 4:30 am daily, and Saturday nights were spent in party mode. She was in her mid-twenties and thought she could do it all.

But something wasn't 100 per cent right with Mariah's health. Regular stress was causing her stomach to feel constantly upset. She was always tired. She didn't ignore it, but she pushed through. Mariah never once thought that the life she was leading was the cause of her illness.

While having regular tests to get to the bottom of her stomach problems and fatigue, Mariah was building her empire. She was spending full days on Zoom calls, creating marketing materials for her clients, and showing up on social media. She was doing all the things she needed to do to build the business that would (in the future) allow her the freedom to travel. It was the 2020 lockdown; what else was she going to do?

Mariah had set her sights on leaving Melbourne for a new life in Sydney before going deeper into her digital nomad dream. In November 2020, she was half-packed. At the same time, she underwent a series of tests to diagnose her health problems. Although her gut told her there was something wrong, she ignored the signs to slow down. Mariah felt she had no reason to worry, but her goal was to get some answers.

Well, the answer was what she got. Her specialist broke the news to her. One tumour on the small bowel. But the prognosis was good. It was benign, and a series of revisions from the St Vincent's Hospital specialist team in Melbourne would determine if it needed to be removed.

This phone call was the beginning of rock bottom for Mariah. She cried and cried that day, feeling like she had failed her body. But work still needed to be done. She 'took it easy', sat on the couch and did the rest of her work. Why was she like this? What was her motivation for working so much? In Mariah's words, it was 'people pleasing'. Always feeling the need to please others. To be enough. These feelings and a lack of self-worth led her to always push herself beyond her limits. Maybe you can relate to these feelings of always wanting to please others. In Mariah's case, where was her story headed?

In the following months, Mariah moved to Sydney as planned. Her medical appointments were handed over to the Sydney St Vincent's team. She went on with life, maintaining the hustle energy, and feeling tired but still pushing. She loved what she did, and her mentality at the time was that she could sleep when she was dead. Little did she know that might have been a reality for her, had she not made the right change at the right time.

That time in Mariah's life was a whirlwind: moving to Sydney, working hard and finally dealing with her health. She was referred to a surgeon to discuss her options—something she thought would be a 2021 issue. Unfortunately, this was not the case. Mariah found herself in a surgeon's office on December 28 2020 to discuss a tumour that, in fact, was two tumours and not benign at all.

Her only option was a Whipple operation—something she had NEVER heard of before but was about to change her life forever. A Whipple operation was performed to cut out suspected cancerous tumours from her small bowel and pancreas. This kind of operation is deemed very dangerous. It would mean the realignment of her digestive system and the removal of half her pancreas, and some of her small bowel and stomach. Her doctors told her she needed six months to recover. 'But what about my clients?!' was the first thing Mariah thought.

**The hardest part about this story—
Mariah was twenty-six.**

Whipple operations are usually performed on people in their sixties or older. It was time for Mariah to start listening to her body, to start listening when her intuition told her to slow down, rest and look after herself. This was a worst-case burnout (and disconnection) scenario.

WHAT IS BURNOUT?

Mariah's story is a dramatic example, but burnout like this is common. While it might not end in a serious health problem, burnout is a worldwide issue that we as entrepreneurs need to become more aware of. Even though we love our businesses, does this need to come at the price of our health?

I have seen dear friends struggle with the same things I did during my burnout *(as you've read about in the introduction).* Some even lost their friends, family and relationships. Some took their lives. This message needs to be shared with the world—and with you.

Unlike a cold or the flu, burnout doesn't hit all at once.

Psychologist Herbert Freudenberger[1] attempted to describe the chronological development of burnout syndrome in a twelve-stage model. It applies to you as a Sacred CEO[2] or an employee in any business. Read through the following steps and note if anything resonates with you. The twelve stages of burnout, according to Freudenberger, are:

1   A compulsion to prove oneself (excessive ambition). It is often found at the beginning to be excessively ambitious. The desire to prove oneself in business, in the workplace, turns into compulsion.

2   Working harder. People establish high personal expectations because they have to prove themselves to others. To meet these expectations, they tend to focus solely on work while taking on more work than they otherwise would.

---

1   Freudenberger, H.J. (1974). Staff burnout. Journal of Social Issues, 30, 159-165

2   I created the concept of Sacred CEO because, if you consider yourself Sacred, you trust yourself as a CEO. The bigger role of the CEO is to hold the vision. In considering yourself sacred, you will not sacrifice your rituals, your well-being, your impact, your team and your community, as you have decided to be at the helm of that vision.

3 Neglecting one's own needs. Since some people must devote everything to work, they have no time and energy for anything else. Friends and family, eating and sleeping start to be seen as unnecessary or unimportant because they reduce the time and energy that can be spent on work.

4 Displacement of conflicts and needs. People become aware that what they're doing isn't right, but they're unable to see the source of the problem. This may lead to a crisis in themselves and become threatening. The first physical symptoms appear.

5 Revision of values. While falling into a state of denial of basic physical needs, perceptions and value systems change. Work consumes all energy, leaving no time for friends and hobbies. The job is the new value system, and people become emotionally blunt.

6 Increasing denial of the problem, decreasing flexibility of thought/behaviour. People may become intolerant and dislike being social. They may be seen as aggressive and sarcastic. Problems may be blamed on time pressure and all the work they must do.

7 Withdrawal, lack of direction, cynicism. Minimal social contact turns into isolation. Alcohol or drugs may be used as a release from obsessive working 'by the book'. These people often have feelings of being without hope or direction.

8   Behavioural changes/psychological reactions. Co-workers, peers, family, friends and others in their immediate social circles can't overlook the behavioural changes in these people.

9   Depersonalisation: loss of contact with self and own needs. It's possible that these people no longer see themselves or others as valuable. Their view of life narrows to only seeing the moment, and life turns into a series of mechanical functions.

10 Inner emptiness, anxiety, addictive behaviour. They feel empty inside and may exaggerate activities such as overeating or sex to overcome these feelings.

11 Increasing feelings of meaninglessness and lack of interest. Burnout may include depression. In that case, the person is exhausted, hopeless, indifferent, and believes life has no meaning.

12 Physical exhaustion, which can be life-threatening. People may collapse physically and emotionally and need immediate medical attention. In extreme cases, suicide may occur, which is viewed as an escape from their situation.

Do any of these feelings resonate? Do you feel tired? Do you feel the mental load and just don't know how to balance yourself? Do you feel like you are running on that hamster wheel? Maybe you have had life coaches, mentors or business coaches who have told you how to direct your life or business. They've told you everything you should do or try, but nothing seems to work.

Remember, we can also suffer from parental and emotional burnout, to name a few other types of burnout. This book is relevant for entrepreneurs specifically, but is also for anyone who would like to reconnect more broadly with their light and get out of burnout and back into harmony.

I am here to tell you the answers are within yourself. I know you've heard that before and maybe you're rolling your eyes now. But I invite you in this book to connect with your intuition to discover these answers step by step.

Right now, it is time to work out where you are at. You can't make the right change if you don't know the problem, right?

So, what? This is not a book solely on burnout. It is a book to help you connect to your intuition and your business/life/self. A book to help you find alignment again and connection so you don't burn out. Just a reminder that you don't always need a breakdown for a breakthrough to happen. But first, become aware of what is happening to you. And why you might feel stuck and unmotivated.

Keep in mind that just because you are feeling disconnected, it doesn't mean your diagnosis is burnout. It might just mean it is time to start nurturing yourself.

WHY DO WE BURN OUT?

You might be thinking, this has started to get dark. But it is not a time for self-diagnosis. It is a time for self-awareness. Remember, these periods happen. If you feel you need to get professional help, please do so. To find yourself and to connect with your intuition, first identify the disconnection. As I mentioned above, it helped me in my own burnout journey.

According to a survey done by Asana in 2021, burnout is rising. Over half (fifty-two per cent) of survey respondents experienced burnout in 2021—up from the forty-three per cent who said the same in Indeed's pre-COVID-19 survey. If you are feeling a bit of burnout or early signs of it, know you are not alone.[3]

Burnout often results from feeling disconnected, disembodied, and unaligned with your path and intuition. But allowing the feeling of being lost and disconnected is important. Imagine it's like allowing your tree to lose its leaves in winter. Although the leaves die when they fall off the tree, the nutrients they give the soil play a part in the birth of new

---

3   https://asana.com/resources/anatomy-of-work

life. It is about allowing the cycle of death for rebirth to happen. In Aboriginal culture, as described in *The Dreaming Path*, Paul Callaghan says, 'It is a cycle of renewal like all things have a cycle of renewal.'

Humans live the same rhythm year after year, following a solar cycle of the seasons, equinoxes and solstices. Changes in the season are evident, and so are the phases of your life. As humans, we are part of the same ecology as all beings, so your body will be influenced by the change of season! We are cyclical, and so is our business.

You may feel at a crossroads in your business and life. You may feel you are running on empty—take this as a signal to pay attention to what needs to happen for you to reconnect.

But why do you feel like this? Here is what I imagine.

You might be trying all the blueprints, life hacks and 'secrets' to business but not getting any results. You have seen them work for others, so why not you too? You might be following a recipe, but you get different results. This is deflating. How can you keep going at the same tempo if you aren't seeing the same results as other people?

Instead of stepping back to listen to what you intuitively know will work in your business, you try a new thing. You 'get back on the horse', as we say. But do you know what happens? You work *more* because you don't believe you are doing enough. You must 'work harder' to get results (so you have been told).

You stay on your computer later at night, skip lunch and the next thing you know, you have worked twelve to fourteen hours and don't know what is working any more. Let's go back to our garden. Some plants need less love and bloom with ease. It doesn't always mean that more work means more results.

If you revisit the twelve stages of burnout, you might identify them with areas of your life right now. Why do we burn out? Because we think there is a recipe for success, but running a business is like raising children. Every child needs different parenting styles, just like different businesses require different strategies. Those strategies don't have to involve doing more. Sometimes they involve doing less. What it really means is connecting with your intuition in the same way parents often do. I was guilty of reading many parenting books before I connected to my intuition as a mother. Your business is born and created out of your womb; it is your baby, and success is about leading it intuitively. Listening to the whisper of your heart and soul as you create, birth and grow it.

WHAT HAPPENS WHEN YOU RECONNECT?

It is time to accept where you are now.

Don't spend this time beating yourself up because you haven't given yourself the love and support you need. If I didn't go through my burnout, I would have never discovered my aligned purpose. I would have never moved to Australia and been doing the work I do now.

The work I feel most aligned with is the type that allows me the freedom to live how I choose. I love waking up each day with the freedom to work as many hours and spend as much time with my family as I want. I don't know where I would be now if I didn't go through my burnout in 2014. I don't want to know. Every decision I made post-burnout was in alignment with what I needed.

I do understand, in the moment of disconnection, when it feels, well—shit—that it is hard to trust your gut. It is hard to surrender. To let go of control, to let go of the 'push harder' mentality. However, I am telling you that when you do let go and trust and follow your intuition, the magic happens. It is time to stop outsourcing your intuition. It is your most unique asset in business and by disconnecting with it you are giving your power away. Reconnect with it, reclaim it, light it like you'll light a candle! You'll thank me later.

The reward? So much more than you could EVER imagine. This feels better than anything—better than sex or Christmas when you were seven years old. And guess what? You get to experience this feeling consistently. Maybe not every minute of every day, but you can tap back into your intuition whenever you need it to give you the answer.

When you reconnect, you get more time with your family, less time at your laptop, and you get your energy back. This energy becomes infectious to those who work with you or want to work with you.

You actually learn to listen to what you want. Not what everyone else wants.

Once you learn this work and what finding your light is all about, you will always be able to return to it. Further along in this book you'll read some powerful stories on what's possible when you reconnect with your intuition, your inner light. But the first step is figuring out where that disconnect began and rebuilding from that point forward.

I know you have it within you. We are all intuitive and light beings. I know you can get this feeling of serene expansion. Enjoy the process. Trust and surrender, dear one.

Remember when I said you are not alone? Well, it isn't just me who has been through these times of stress, of feeling lost and disconnected. I am not the only one who has felt like their body (or mind) is 'failing'. Many people on this planet have gone through exactly what you're going through now.

FROM DIAGNOSIS TO RECONNECTION

So, you might be wondering what happened to Mariah, whose story I shared at the beginning of this chapter? On March 2 2021, Mariah went to St Vincent's Hospital in Sydney and had her Whipple operation—the removal of half her pancreas, and part of her stomach and bowel. Her recovery was slow (eighteen months in total), but she didn't need chemo because the surgeon got all the tumours. However, the tumours had missed her lymph nodes by a fraction. She was lucky and learned many lessons from her scary health experience. Moving forward, she was always honest with her clients and listened to her intuition. Instead of the 'she'll be alright' mentality I see a lot in countries like Australia, Mariah took her time to heal.

When Mariah finally left the hospital four weeks after her surgery, it didn't mean she returned to the scheduled program. She made dramatic changes in her life. She invested in herself rather than just her business. Not only that, she reflected on what she really wanted in life.

She wanted to be loved (she was single at the time), and she wanted to travel (because she realised life was too short). Mariah started her business in pursuit of being a digital nomad. While COVID saw that change, she didn't make the lifestyle choices associated with being a nomad. She didn't go outside much; she spent a lot of time inside on her laptop.

Mariah's health scare sent her back on the path to her vision. Guess what happened when she finally got back on track? Just six months later, she met her soul mate, who always wanted to be a digital nomad and had marketing qualifications just like she did. As I write this book, Mariah is travelling around Australia in the back of an SUV with her partner. She still works on her business and loves serving her clients, but she does it in a way that feels good. However, she had to make those choices. She had to do the work.

Mariah changed her content marketing agency model to look like a consultancy-based business. She stepped into the pricing model she was worth and made time for herself. When she made time for herself, even just some quiet time throughout the day, it allowed her to listen to what she really wanted, not what she heard all around her. Not what she thought she needed for her life and business.

You will be happy to know Mariah is still cancer free two years after her operation and is in the best health she has ever been! She puts it down to connecting with herself and listening to what she needs. She has been a private client since her diagnosis and I am honoured to be by her side as she deepens her connection with her intuition over time.

KNOW YOURSELF MORE

Now it is your turn to see where you are at. Where on your journey do you stand? This is a time to reflect without judgement. Just be aware, fully present and identify. Know you are not alone.

It's time to figure out how you currently feel. The following questions will give you an honest picture of your current life. You can find them in your workbook or download them at www.lightitbook.com. Remember that you can feel disconnected from different areas of your life. You might feel disconnected from yourself, your kids, work, friends, clients or relationships. But for the purpose of this book, we are focusing on your business.

Go through the following questions and tick the box if it describes you. Remember, keep an open mind (welcoming all the thoughts) and your heart wide (welcoming all the feelings) as you go through this. It is about connecting with your greater emotional intelligence and developing heartfelt listening skills.

This opening process is important as an individual or collective (remember that we are all connected). Be compassionate, soft and gentle with yourself and with those around you. It is all about bringing awareness. This self-assessment does not replace a specialist's help. It is about empowering you to know yourself.

Here are the questions. If the answer is 'yes', put a tick in the box:

○ **I feel exhausted.** Feeling physically and emotionally depleted. Physical symptoms may include headaches, stomach aches, change of appetite, disrupted sleep or insomnia.

○ **I feel disengaged.** Being unmotivated to engage in activities that you usually love. Being willing to stop socialising and confiding in loved ones and others. We will speak later about the different areas of parenting, work, social life, and more.

○ **I feel resentful.** When you are disconnected from your true self, your intuition, it can cause you to lose your cool with loved ones and others. Coping with normal stressors like preparing for a work meeting, driving kids to school, and doing household tasks may feel insurmountable, especially when things don't go as planned.

○ **I suffer from frequent illnesses**. Burnout, like other long-term stress, can lower your immune system, making you more susceptible to colds, the flu and insomnia. It can also lead to mental health concerns like depression and anxiety.

Take your time. Look at these questions and decide if you need to sit with them. Remember, this is your experience.

If you are reading this, you have done the assessment and you want to talk about it, please feel free to reach out to me on Instagram @essential.shift (www. instagram.com/essential.shift/).

If you answered 'yes' to most of these, you might not have burnout, but you are probably experiencing some disconnection in your life. I recommend you see a medical professional for diagnosis.

You might be disconnected from your intuition or body if you answered 'yes' to some of these. Maybe you are just looking for outside validation, tips and tricks for your business. Still, you have everything you need within you to build your own business. Stay on your own path and embrace your unique intuitive nudges. The world has just begun.

KEY MESSAGES

- Burnout is real and often referred to as the plague of this century.

- Psychologist Herbert Freudenberger has defined the twelve stages of burnout to help identify where people are in their burnout journey.

- Bringing awareness—paying attention—to which level of burnout you're at can help you heal.

- Healing is possible, and it is a journey of reconnection to your light.

- You are not alone; others have had the same experience. With a little work, you and others like you can live in true alignment.

2

INTUITION TO BE BLISSED OUT INSTEAD OF BURNED OUT

STOP DOING AND START LISTENING

When I started my business, I chose not to run it like I ran my strategy consulting job when I lived in Paris. Working like that led me to be clinically diagnosed as burned out. Instead, I wanted to be blissed out. I wanted to enjoy time with my family, my two daughters and my husband. I wanted to travel back to France (which I have done every year since going all-in with my business) to see family without feeling like I was 'too busy'.

**I wanted to go out for coffee with my
girlfriends or take a walk on the beach
without feeling like I needed
to be back at my laptop working.**

I built this habit from day one of working full-time in my business. Instead of launching multiple programs at once and overworking myself, I spent my first day as a full-time entrepreneur at a cooking class with my five-year-old daughter. I will always remember her smile when she saw me entering her classroom. I spent the morning with my eldest and her classmates. This was something I never got to do when I worked in corporate. From then on, I set boundaries with myself and my business because those things were important.

You might be thinking, well, that's a good way to have slow business growth. But actually, the opposite happened.

I made over six figures within the first seven months of starting my business. I know this is a big deal because the statistics say so. Did you know (according to The Women's Business Enterprise National Council) that eighty-eight per cent of women-owned businesses make less than $100,000 in revenue annually?[4] These were my results in seven months! I put it down to this...

---

4   https://earthweb.com/women-entrepreneurs-statistics/

- Intuition, and trusting myself and the process
- Strategy and vision
- Showing up for my community and myself

It didn't happen from working 24/7, pouring money into Facebook ads, or following a blueprint or secret recipe. Honestly, it was my intuition. It was trusting and knowing what I needed to do for my business. Not for anyone else's business, but for my own. I'm not saying here that reaching $100,000 in revenue needs to be your goal. Still, I'm telling you that it is possible without burning out, dropping everything and quitting your business. Because according to research by Fundera, approximately twenty per cent of small businesses fail within the first year. By the end of the second year, only thirty per cent of businesses will have failed. By the end of the fifth year, about half will have failed. And by the end of the decade, only thirty percent of businesses will remain—a seventy per cent failure rate.[5] How many fail because of burnout? I wonder...

People have always asked me how I managed to achieve all these things in such a short time, and it was actually from doing less rather than more. I will always tell my team that I need to Honour my teachings and go outside when I feel stuck, take care of my own needs when I feel neglected and trust myself when I have an idea.

---

5   https://www.entrepreneur.com/starting-a-business/
the-true-failure-rate-of-small-businesses/361350

> **We can all do the same. We just need to trust our intuition.**

WHAT IS INTUITION?

Intuition can be felt through the body's response, such as a 'gut feeling', a heart expansion or a sense of knowing.

How do you know if what you're feeling is intuition or not? Just ask yourself the following questions:

- Are you rationalising this decision?

- Do you feel you need to search for the answer outside of yourself?

- Do you feel a sense of anxiety with this choice you have?

If the answer is 'no' to most of these questions, it's your intuition you are feeling.

Let's say you get a 'feeling' you need to change what you are doing in business. Perhaps it's a nudge to change an offering or remove a current offering.[6]

Think about the words you use around it and how it comes to your mind.

---

6   We use the word 'offering' here to encompass anything you sell in your business. It can be a product, a service, a SaaS.

If you say things like: 'I feel...', 'I know...', 'I believe...', this sounds like your intuition.

If an idea comes to you out of nowhere, and you just know you have to do it, this is intuition.

But if you have ideas in your head that could have come from external sources and your language is 'I think...', 'I should...', 'I could...', this is not intuition.

Remember, your intuition is a muscle. When you start to notice it, it will continue to grow. The more you listen to it, the bigger it gets.

When you connect with your intuition, you connect to LIGHT. This means darkness is easier to get through because you are guided in the right direction. It doesn't mean there will be no darkness; it just means that, guided by your intuition, you will find the light easier. The light is your vision guided by intuition. What you want. Why you are here. Your purpose.

Your business is closely linked to your purpose, so we must ensure our intuition is always trusted.

WHY INTUITION IN BUSINESS?

When we don't use our intuition in our business and if we don't connect with ourselves, it is like having a big head with no body and no heart. So, this leads me to one quick question to help you understand why we should use intuition in business. If you only thought with your head, how would you carry it?

With any garden, you must give it time and trust the process. That is what you need to do when you run a business backed by your intuition.

My business logo has three connected circles. These represent the heart, body and mind.

We connect with the heart (which represents intuition), the body (which represents action) and the mind (which represents strategy). When we connect these together, it creates harmony in our business.

But it doesn't mean it must always be split into equal parts. Let's use launching a new offering as an example of how I would use the heart, body and mind in business:

The first thing I need to start with is the heart. I make space to listen to this intuition and the needed guidance. This is how I built my course 'Ayurveda in Business'. You might be thinking, what is Ayurveda? And how does ancient wisdom work in a business?

Ayurveda's origin is in India and can be translated to mean the 'Science of Life' (ayur = life, veda = science) and is often referred to as 'Mother of All Healing.' Indeed, it is considered by many scholars to be the oldest healing science. It has deep roots in ancient Vedic tradition.

Ayurveda is a holistic science, an art of living that addresses all aspects of life, including the body, mind and emotions. Ayurveda has been a journey of deep self-discovery for me since living in India in 2004 and it has allowed me to connect with my body, mind and heart to intuitively harmonise my imbalances in life and business. I felt the calling to share more about it to unlock this knowledge for others.

From this intuitive nudge came expansion, a knowing and feeling in my heart that was growing. A moment of whole-body agreement. Side note, I often tell people, if it is not a full body yes, then it is a no! From there, I could see this offering opening up. I could see it moving forward, and I knew it was what I needed to create.

Then I asked, why am I creating it? At the time, I felt Ayurveda in Business was needed to help entrepreneurs apply ancient spiritual wisdom to grow their businesses sustainably, in alignment with their unique energy (called *dosha*[7] in Ayurveda). I believed (and still believe) it would be impactful for all entrepreneurs on the verge of burning out to connect with their own *dosha* in business. I know it is unique. The next thing for me was validating this offer with more logic and what I knew about my ideal customer, my ideal avatar. This is how I bring my mind. My mind

---

7   Ayurveda explains that each of us inherits a unique metabolic constitution that shapes our mental, physical and emotional tendencies. There are three principles called doshas—Vata, Pitta, Kapha—that blend together to determine our metabolic type.

comes in to think of the strategy and to answer the question: what does it look like?

Then how I will put this new offering together is provided by my body. How will I create content to launch it? How will the course be delivered? What will be the price point, and so on. You can learn more about the 'Ayurveda in Business' course, the only course in the world teaching how to apply Ayurveda to your business, and join anytime on my website www.essentialshift.co. You will experience deep transformation in the way you run your business, just like hundreds of program alumni.

For yourself, it can be in another order, but all three parts of body, mind and heart come together. And I truly believe it needs to start from the heart space, from the intuition. After that moment of inner knowing, you might go to the strategy (mind) or the action (body).

For example, a creative person might go from the heart to the body to start creating what they visualised.

There also might be times when more heart is involved, or more of the body or the head plays a role. But as I mentioned, they all work together from the heart.

Think about how we make bold moves or courageous moves as well. Do you think if we used our head and the strategy mind, we would make those bold moves? No way. You would never make a bold move from your head. You make them from your intuition. Because a blueprint won't get you there.

Side note here—the word courage comes from the Old French word 'corage', which derives from the Latin word 'cor', meaning heart. Amazing, right?

Let us explore a courageous move and how intuition links to that.

The Founder of the company Patagonia, Yvon Chouinard, made the definition of a courageous move in his business. One we can only describe as something that came from a true intuitive nudge.

Yvon Chouinard gave away his $3 billion business (Patagonia) to the climate justice movement, a non-profit called the Holdfast Collective.

While most people would think he was crazy, this action aligned with his vision. He started Patagonia to help protect the planet, so giving his business away to a climate change non-profit seems like an intuitive nudge. There is no perceivable logic in this because there was no clear monetary gain, but from what I can imagine, he knew he needed to do it. Time will tell what it means.

While this is an extreme case of intuition and bold moves, and you might not relate to that decision, you can understand the courage and boldness he must have felt when he made that move.

WHAT HAPPENS WHEN YOU CONNECT TO INTUITION IN YOUR BUSINESS?

When you connect with your intuition in business, you stop hustling. You don't have to work twelve-hour days. You feel more worthy and less guilty. You prevent burnout and feel blissed out.

From what I have seen happen in these moments of connection to intuition, people fall back in love with their business.

Instead of lying in bed each morning unsure what to do in your business, you spring out of bed certain of what lies ahead.

Instead of worrying about where your next sale will come from, your business grows. You reclaim your right to be the Sacred CEO of your business and not the nine-to-five worker. You get holidays and time with your family. Actually, life is a holiday!

You give yourself permission to take time off! You trust yourself more to grow the business you have been dreaming about!

You have this sense of harmony between your life and your business. You set the boundaries you want and always have that awareness of when you are doing too much.

You might even:

- Spring out of bed, ready for the day

- Spend time with your family in the morning

- Go for a walk or do something in the morning that fills up your cup

- Work on the most important things of the day

- Take lunch NOT at your desk

- Do more work in the afternoon (if you want to or need to)

- Finish before 5 pm and enjoy a cup of tea and some time to yourself before dinner

- Spend the evening with your family

You have days off mid-week and get to focus on the tasks you like to do, because your intuition will tell you not to do the tasks you don't like or find a solution to get them done. You trust yourself more, which means your energy is infectious. People love working with others who have infectious energy.

The cycle continues. You get off that hamster wheel and build your business, not the business that doesn't work for you. If you don't believe it is possible, let me share a case study on how this has become a reality for a business owner you might relate to.

MOVING FROM DISCONNECTION TO RECONNECTION AND INTUITION IN BUSINESS

NAME: Jessica Tutton, Australia
BUSINESS: Launch and
Facebook™ ads strategist

As the owner of an online business, Jessica Tutton lost her spark. She had a lot of success and was doing everything right but working too much. While earning hundreds of thousands in her business and working with successful clients, she wasn't happy.

Jessica lost her connection to her vision, to herself and to why she started an online business. She disconnected from the voice in her heart that said, 'You are doing too much,' and kept going. This made her feel depleted in business and unsure of her next step. But she had this inner knowing that she needed to change it all. Almost burn it to the ground and start again. From the outside looking in, this seemed crazy. But her heart (intuition) was telling her to make a change.

We worked with Jessica to help her connect to her intuition and what she wanted to do. Not what society said she should do or what she thought she should be doing. The first thing we did was an exercise of self-inquiry to help her decide what she was passionate about in her business and what she was not so passionate about. We reconnected with her heart and intuition and used it again as her compass to guide her in her decisions moving forward. It was a process to trust, but she realised what she wanted when we reconnected with her why and her vision using her intuition as a guide. Jessica realised she created her business to be with her family and experience a nomadic lifestyle, but she wasn't living that truth. From there, she redesigned her business. Jessica refined her definition of success. She wasn't attached to the things she had created. It didn't make sense rationally, but it made sense intuitively to make space and re-create a more aligned business and lifestyle.

Not even twelve months later, Jessica had completely connected back. She let go of parts of her business that didn't allow her to return to her vision. This wasn't a quick (or easy) process. It meant letting go and revamping her systems to allow for more freedom-based offerings, all things that might not have made sense at the time. But it was all worth it.

Jessica also connected back to why she started her business (and her intuition). Everything aligned, and Jessica is now living life on her terms. She started to design her life around where she saw herself and her family. She found her light, her passion for business. As I write this book she has been travelling around Australia for over six months with her family (husband and three young kids) in a campervan and doesn't know yet when the trip will end. She is loving this freedom-based lifestyle that her business allows her and when we caught up in person during her visit in Sydney she told me that she rediscovered her mojo in business thanks to the work we did.

Jessica Tutton is living in true
alignment and trusting her intuition
to grow her business in a way that
doesn't sacrifice herself or her family.

PUTTING IT INTO PRACTICE
CONNECT WITH YOUR INTUITION

Here is a simple way to connect with your intuition right now to better understand how it works. Flip a coin!

Whatever answer it lands on, be mindful of how you feel. If disappointed, your intuition guides you to the other option or answer.

If you feel at peace, it is the right answer.
It doesn't have to be rocket science
right now. This is just an easy way to
understand what your intuition is.

You can use this simple exercise to understand how your intuition works. Just like going to the gym, your intuition is a muscle we must build on. In the next chapter, I will introduce you to the five steps that will truly and deeply help you connect with your intuition, so you never scramble through your purse or the house to find a coin.

Are you ready for the next steps? Read on to Chapter Three!

KEY MESSAGES

- We are all intuitive beings. It is just about connecting with ourselves daily to build that trust again.

- In business (and in life more generally), connecting with the heart (which represents intuition), the body (which represents action) and the mind (which represents strategy) creates harmony.

- Make space and embrace the void to connect with your intuition.

PART 2

THE LIGHT FRAMEWORK EXPLAINED

BEFORE GETTING INTO the LIGHT, let me tell you how this book and framework were channelled through me. As I mentioned briefly in the introduction, this book journey started when I was grieving my friend who died suddenly from cancer in his early thirties. He left behind his wife and two young kids, all feeling lost.

We used to work together in strategy consulting when I burned out, which reminds me that it could have killed me.

As I was grieving his loss and supporting his wife and family, I decided to go on a solo retreat. I was in a deep meditative state, or trance state. The universe told me I needed to write a book and teach as many people as possible the LIGHT framework.

As the message came, I asked, 'What is the LIGHT?' The answer that I kept receiving was, 'you know it!' I could see my boundless light shining bright and other lights around me. I felt lighter and lighter, I connected with my inner light, my intuition, and I knew what it was. For many years, I unconsciously applied the philosophy in this book, but now it is time to name it, package it and share it with all of you so you can apply it consciously to your business (and life).

So even if writing a book was never on my bucket list, I followed my own light, my intuitive self and started writing this book.

It hasn't been an easy process. I went back to the LIGHT framework as I was writing this book. Each step was honoured multiple times. Applying LIGHT to your life is a powerful cyclical process because everything is cyclical. Writing a book and being a published author didn't make sense and still doesn't, but does it have to make sense? No, because this is how intuition feels!

I tested the framework during multiple workshops and Business Birthing Retreats to iterate and validate it before sharing it with you in this book. I hope you'll enjoy it as much as the participants of those events did. I look forward to seeing you apply it to your business and, more broadly, to all aspects of your life. Remember: all is connected.

The LIGHT framework is my unique process. It is for impact-driven entrepreneurs (you) to grow a soul-aligned business and go way beyond surface-level success. Embodying my LIGHT framework allows business owners like you to use your intuition to make the right choices uniquely to you.

You'll learn the power of Leaning in, Illuminating, Gathering, Honouring and Transforming and discover a new way of running a business, which will help you create a business by design.

There are five steps we will look at:

- **Lean in**—gives you the strength to explore the triquetra past, present and future and to go after your vision.

- **Illuminate**—allows you to look at the path forward to align with your vision and learn your next steps to business (or life) alignment.

- **Gather**—asks you for a two-way sense of Gathering: Gathering within (who you are and where you are coming from) and Gathering with (who you know and the community you belong to). It is about bringing everything together.

- **Honour**—is about accepting. It is knowing not everything will go to plan as you want it to. It is about knowing you have done the work.

- **Transform**—is all about your rebirth. You are a new version of yourself. You became the person you need to be to achieve what you set out to achieve. No matter how big or small it was.

This part of the book breaks down the LIGHT framework into bite-sized pieces for you to have a roadmap to reconnecting daily with your intuition in business. It is a cyclical and iterative process.

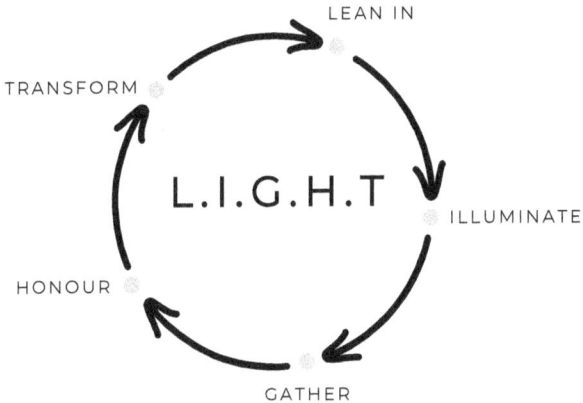

Figure 2.1. The LIGHT framework, iterative and cyclical by Laetitia Andrac

3

LEAN IN

THOSE WHO LEAN INTO BUSINESS INTUITION

While researching well-known entrepreneurs and reading the stories of many, I came across a lot of amazing business owners who use their intuition to help them 'Lean in' to what they want to create in their business. They use intuition to help them decide what is next—what to sell, what to offer and who to help. One of them is Richard Branson. As he mentions in his business blog, he has always relied on his intuition when taking calculated risks in business. He has always trusted people around him to make business decisions. I imagine he chose those people based on his intuition too. A beautiful quote from this article reads: 'Trust your intuition, stay curious, and always put your people first if you want to thrive in the long term.'[8] So if Richard Branson can run a billion-dollar business using intuition, so can you! There is another entrepreneur who stands out to me. Let's talk about...

Samantha Wills, who is an Australian entrepreneur, author and other amazing things. Samantha was the owner of Samantha Wills Jewellery. She did the hustle of being in business and built up a successful jewellery label from this space. She started in her kitchen and built a global empire. Her success on its own is a beautiful and inspiring story.

While editing my book, I came across Samantha's story through her book, *Of Gold and Dust*.[9] She mentioned her intuitive feelings when in business, and from there, my intuition told me, 'Add Samantha to the book.' Even though I already had a great story, my intuition told me this was important.

Samantha's hustle in business became toxic, to the point that she had health issues. She required major surgery for chronic endometriosis. She says in her book, 'Burnout is the result of an excessive and ongoing imbalance.' She explained that before her major surgery, her advice on 'how to avoid burnout' would have been very different from now. Her advice in her book was to 'understand the importance of boundaries, personal well-being and self-care.'

---

8 https://www.virgin.com/branson-family/richard-branson-blog/instinct-world-analytics

9 https://samanthawills.com/book

Again, something she wouldn't have said before her health scare.

So, you might be wondering, what was Samantha's journey? How did she use her intuition? Her intuition called her to do something very bold.

She closed her global jewellery empire...

She received an email from her business partner, Geoff, while she was on a road trip for a weekend getaway; the subject line read 'Business at a crossroads.' Samantha explained that her inner voice told her as soon as she saw that email, 'Close the business.'

This was her intuition. Her heart wasn't in it any more.

As she explains in her book, intuition is an instant knowing, a feeling of calm. One that logic can't describe. One that the ego won't understand.

At that moment, she didn't trust her intuition fully. While calling for a sign to move forward with her decision, she was presented with the book *Big Magic* by Elizabeth Gilbert (a book I love dearly). The book was given to her at a university bookstore on her road trip. You can't make this stuff up.

Big Magic brought all her fears to light. It helped her question what was next so she could explore who Samantha Wills really was without this famous jewellery empire.

She did it. She closed her business. She didn't tell a soul for two weeks, but she emailed her business partner and made the decision. She couldn't sell the brand because it was built on her and her name.

While reading the final chapters of her book, she talked about the soul and how it is guided to make the choices that challenge us. Leaning in and having faith in your intuition will lead you where you need to go. While the ego will want you to stay where you are, your soul will be guided by the unfamiliar.

Samantha shared her experience of holding on tight and listening to what her body told her. Closing her business was a nudge, one would say, a scary nudge. When she declared her vision, a 'Lean in' moment helped her take that next step forward. While Samantha calls it faith, I call it 'Lean in'.

She followed a gut feeling to share her amazing achievements and show others the power of tapping into what your soul (your intuition) is calling for. She decided to do this by writing a business memoir.

To Lean in might not mean completely uprooting your business or life. It could look like moving forward to the unknown that doesn't make logical sense. This path didn't make sense to Samantha at the time. But her health, her need to stay abroad (and not move back to Australia) and her vision to start something new called her to Lean in. It called her to let go of something old and start something new.

Beautiful, right?

WHAT IT MEANS TO 'LEAN IN'

Coming on this journey of connecting to your intuition in business is about starting with the first step, Lean in. Lean in represents the 'L' in the LIGHT framework.

Leaning in is about sitting at the table and working towards the vision you created when you first wanted to be an entrepreneur. If you don't have a vision yet, that's okay. This chapter will help you connect with yours.

Have you heard of the work from Sheryl Sandberg (ex-COO of Meta/Facebook)? If not, I invite you to read her book: *Lean In: Women, Work, and the Will to Lead*. *Lean In* has become a catchphrase for empowering women. Indeed, it is all about showing women how, if you take a seat at the table, you are Leaning into what you offer, to your uniqueness.

This is how I see it.

Leaning in is about stepping up and becoming the Sacred CEO. It is the moment when you jump into the deeper water and become ready for the next step. The next iteration of your business. Creating the business of your dreams backed by your vision.

Finally, it is also about trust. When you jump from the top of the mountain, know your parachute will guide you, like Samantha Wills did. Her jump off that mountain was closing a multimillion-dollar business, and guess what? That parachute led her to many opportunities.

The Lean in of your journey is about opening the door, remembering your past, being present and trusting the future.

This is what I love to explain to my clients. The first step is BE, then DO and finally, HAVE. It all starts with Leaning in towards your own energy, your own story, your own family and generational story, your own talents, your own life, your own dream and work experiences, your own insights, your own professional training and degrees, accomplishments, team, network/audience, intellectual property. The first step in the method is to BE intentionally aligned with your vision. Being intentional means standing in communion with your past, present and future.

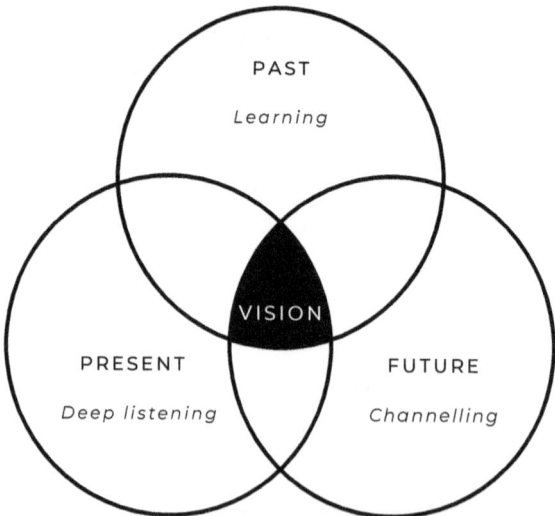

Figure 3.1. Vision Triquetra by Laetitia Andrac

Yet too many people only focus on one element of the triquetra: past, present or future. As a result, we often get distracted. The three are interconnected and essential to start your journey towards deep alignment. Let me simplify this in a generic table that follows to help you reflect personally on where you may be Leaning in the most.

How to Lean into the past, present and future

When you only Lean into the past	When you only Lean into the present	When you only Lean into the future
EXAMPLE: When your attention and thinking are trapped in regrets of what happened in the past, replaying family or work conflicts, you think about what you could have said or should have said, or what others could have said. You get stuck in the past. Know that some of those are inherited from previous generations. You are drawn away from your light, from what's wanting to emerge.	EXAMPLE: When your attention is fully in the present moment, you are immersed in the task. You are drawn away from the future to bring it into the now. The lessons of the past can help you connect with the light now. You are fully present, which is great. Still, you are not exploring the richness of your past, your ancestral lineage, your experiences or what is emerging in the future.	EXAMPLE: When you keep only worrying about tomorrow, next month, next year, the next five years and so on, you lose your connection to the present moment— which is the only opportunity we have to connect with reality and the ability to act and create this future vision we have. You also lose your connection to your past and all the powerful lessons and transmissions you've gathered. The future is not here yet.
GIFT: Learning	GIFT: Deep listening	GIFT: Channelling
PRACTICE TO TRY: Cultivate the capacity to Lean into the past, to attend to the past in a way that keeps sight of your role in what happened yesterday.	PRACTICE TO TRY: Cultivate the capacity to be fully present and listen deeply to what is willing to emerge from the future in the present moment while Leaning into the lessons from the past.	PRACTICE TO TRY: Cultivate the capacity for sensing and Leaning into the unknown, the space of possibility around us that wants to emerge or that could happen.

Those three elements are connected in your vision for yourself, your business and, more broadly, your life. It invites a deep connection from the past, in the present, to the emerging future.

Focus on your vision with powerful intentionality to the point of obsession. No matter the outcome, failure or success. You are learning either way. When you say yes to the vision, you are saying yes to the vision shaping you. You are saying yes to the emerging light, your intuitive self, who you are. For example, imagine your vision is to be a digital nomad. Maybe that vision comes from being inspired by other successful entrepreneurs in your lineage, in your community, who are digital nomads (learning from the past). So, you focus on that vision for the future you are creating for your business from the beginning to allow you freedom and flexibility. But along the journey of growing your business, you might lose track of it and start creating offerings and taking on clients that make for more work. You find yourself chained to your desk and have no time for travel. But suppose you stay connected daily in the present to the vision, remembering why you started your business. In that case, you Lean in to create more offerings to help you live this lifestyle. You begin to BE the digital nomad now and can explain why you wanted it in the past. Then you DO and HAVE it.

This is NOT the time to know how you will build this offering or business. It is about Why you want it. Start to Lean into what business you want to create based on your vision. You don't have to know the answers right now. But it is time to stand on your box and voice What you need.

Most of the time, our vision doesn't put us in a box. We are so far out of the box we need to turn it upside down and stand on it! When you Lean in, you preach it to the world! When we think of light, it is boundless. It can't fit in a box. See yourself as this light; you are the light.

It is time to step into your sovereignty, put the crown on your head and shine with all your light. BE who you want to become. I often invite my clients to be Sacred CEOs. The role of the CEO is to hold the vision. This means you are ready to embrace that vision and allow it to grow. You are taking responsibility for that vision. You're stepping into your light, being in the spotlight. The vision within you right now informed by your past is also a path forward. The sacred triquetra—past, present and future—is here again.

Try to say it aloud now as you Lean in: 'I am the Sacred CEO of [insert the name of your business].'

This is a potent exercise for many of my clients. By claiming the sacredness of their role as a leader they also claim their vision, and their seat at the table in the present.

WHY YOU MUST LEAN IN

When you Lean into your vision, you learn to trust yourself. That is the process. To Lean in doesn't mean you will have the answers on how you will get from A to B. It is about making the promise to yourself, your clients and your business that the path will be aligned and that you will work towards Why you started your business.

This is important because life won't always go as you wish. I think back to my own experience of Lean in when I wanted to go all-in with Essential Shift and quit my full-time job. This intention was deeply rooted in the past, in the present and in the emerging future. I called it my 'Mission to March' (my plan to exit my job in March 2021). I didn't have a plan, but I had the vision in September 2020 to become the Sacred CEO of Essential Shift by March 2021.

Before I explain more, let me show you how this vision was deeply rooted in the past, present and future. In the past, it was built from my dream to be an entrepreneur. I did a master's degree in entrepreneurship, started my businesses (all three of which failed, plus one I started in business school), and was connected to a family of farmers (who are, in essence, entrepreneurs deeply connected to the cycle of Nature). I set this Mission to March to be ready for the future. I wanted to go all-in with my business and impact entrepreneurs worldwide with my work.

During my Mission to March, my business had low cash flow months. I had offers to partner with large consulting firms with big financial packages that were way more than my business gave me then. There were tests and challenges.

That is why you must Lean in. When you Lean in, you give 111 per cent. You trust the process and know any opportunity is a test or challenge from the universe. Do you want to BE that new version of yourself now to match your vision?

The process of Leaning in is about going all-in. You might have heard the saying, 'Don't put all your eggs in one basket,' but when you have a vision and find the light, it is all about putting your eggs in one basket. When you do, you reap the rewards.

Think about the journey from burnout and disconnection to seeing your wildest dreams come true. The only way to achieve that is to Lean in, to trust that you can bring your vision to life. That vision is the one we are going to reconnect with in this chapter!

During my Business Birthing Retreat, when I guided entrepreneurs through the LIGHT framework, I witnessed that many of them struggled with trusting the vision that was coming up. This is when it is powerful to face your fears and declare your vision. It is a sign that you are no longer willing to play small. This is the bravest move forward. You must commit to it because there will be tests and challenges whether you commit or not. These will prevent you from living truly connected to the Source.

So why should you Lean in at 111 per cent? Because you have no other choice unless you want things to stay the way they are. Unless you want to lack consistency. Consistency will help drive you to where you want to be. To the place you have been longing for.

What does life look like when you don't Lean in? It looks the same way it does now. You continue to work all hours of the day. You miss dinner with your family because you are working. You never take holidays because you don't have time. You forget why you started your business, and instead of working to live, you live to work.

If you feel stuck in business, like you have plateaued and are unsure where to go next, that vision and the Lean in process aren't happening. Maybe you lost sight of your vision; that happens when we get to 'doing all the things' rather than connecting with ourselves. Remember, the first step is BE, DO, and finally, HAVE. Way too many entrepreneurs start with DO.

When we Lean in, we begin finding and reconnecting with our light, but we also start to work towards the business and the life we have always dreamed of.

SHINE YOUR LIGHT
ON ONE THING

Leaning in can give you more than you could ever imagine. It gives you the strength to surrender and the willpower of trust. I had three failed businesses, plus one in business school. At twenty-one, I was doing an entrepreneurship challenge, so I made a board game to help children learn foreign languages. I created it with my peers, but I'm not counting this one as a failure because we never really launched it.

Let me share a bit more about my first real business venture. The one I created when I arrived in Australia, completely lost after my burnout, was called Chef Up. I said yes to the opportunity to create, with two girlfriends, a marketplace for chefs to go to the houses of everyday people and cook for them. There have been super successful startups built on that idea. It failed because I didn't trust my intuition. From the beginning, I resisted Leaning into the feelings that I didn't have the right business partner because we did not share the same vision. I tried to make it work until we realised it simply would not, but I learned from there onward to not ignore my own vision in business.

After that, I created a food-based business with a friend in 2015 called 'Food Is All'. I knew by then that my vision was not in the food industry, but I still ignored my intuition and my vision. Quickly, we realised that I was not as passionate as my co-founder, so I left to preserve our friendship and let her grow the business. She used the name for the business for quite some time before launching her own business in the food industry. It was more her vision than mine. But that's okay because with this failure and experience, I learned that my zone of genius is to help others birth their vision for business.

This caused me to create the third business, which started in 2018, with a long-time friend called Neoma. It was all about supporting mothers through matrescence,[10] finding their purpose and mission, and aligning their careers. It was a step closer to my vision: helping other women birth their businesses. We had to stop the business when my friend planned to leave Australia and go back to France in 2019.

Each failure brought me closer to connecting to my vision and, finally, totally Leaning in with Essential Shift. Every time you fail, you get closer to feeling connected to your vision. Do you remember the triquetra I mentioned before? Past/present/future. These business failures were all part of my journey, leading me to where I needed to be. They led me to my light. I always wanted my own business; I knew it would allow me the freedom I wanted and the ability to impact many others. The vision I had was to create a business.

My vision for Essential Shift is this: to impact one million women by 2032 and to build a world where these women can avoid burning out while growing their million-dollar businesses.

When you Lean in, you get so much more than you think. But more importantly, you find clarity and

---

10 The word and meaning of 'matrescence' was first described in the 1970s by Dana Raphael. But it was recently that matrescence was brought to life again by Dr Aurelie Athan from Columbia University. The stage of matrescence is a beautiful, groundbreaking and revolutionary way to understand what occurs when a woman becomes a mother. Dr Aurelie Athan first described matrescence as being like adolescence. It is a time in a woman's life when everything changes and her whole identity shifts.

purpose. You become laser-focused on what you want. You become intentional, and it all starts with intention. You see one thing: your vision. Think of a lighthouse streaming light on one thing at a time. Just like putting your 'eggs in one basket', connecting with your vision allows you to guide the way forward. The lighthouse has the most impact when it shines its light. This is how you create laser focus and Lean in.

You then bring in the other goals that make up your vision. These goals allow you to bring LIGHT into your life and put you on the path to your legacy, just like the lighthouse focuses on other areas around it, from land to sea. I had moments of this when looking to buy a house, write this book, become a mother and launch my business.

But the first step before I did anything was to Lean in, declare it, be it and trust it would happen for me.

What Leaning in does is give you the focus you need to show yourself you can achieve anything. You can always give yourself what you need and have the answers within yourself.

We see the light, and then we Lean into the light. When we have tilted into the light, the light will Illuminate. We will dive into that in the next chapter on finding your light, 'Illuminate'.

CREATING AN ONLINE BUSINESS WITH INTUITION BY LEANING IN

NAME: Emma Irwin, Australia
BUSINESS: Beauty therapist
and CEO of Your Time Skin Care

Emma Irwin started to Lean into her vision when she started her own business. But it wasn't just about business.

Before that, she was suffering from anxiety. She took this as a sign to take the leap of faith and Lean into her business and her health. She trusted herself to wean off antidepressants and launch an online store for her skincare label during the pandemic.

Both of these actions required a lot of strength. She had a lot of trust in herself, and the journey was about Leaning into where she wanted her life to go because she knew there was more for her to give.

Practising spiritual rituals (such as breathwork and journaling) and calling on mentors helped her when she needed to calm her body and return to herself. But for Emma, it was also about giving herself advice and Leaning into what she knew. We all have the answers within us.

When she took this leap, her business grew.

Launching her skin care range in 2021 was scary, and Emma needed to Lean in.

She invested her own money to create her business. Now she has her own brand. Her own skin care label.

She started selling skin care products in her salon, but when COVID hit, she hired me as her mentor to help her Lean into her vision and launch an online store.

We worked on her coming out of the spiritual closet and Leaning completely into her gifts. A unique feature of her skin care brand was that it was infused with crystal and her reiki healing. She feared her neighbour's judgement because she lived in a small town in a regional area of Australia. But we removed those mindset blocks. We connected with the big vision. We established a clear business strategy to go to market, launched the online store and gathered her contacts. When she discovered later that she has ADHD, she also leaned in to let me help her grow her business with ADHD. When I asked for permission to share her story, she told me to add this to the book: 'Leaning into challenges with my ADHD diagnosis—and your teachings and support around this and watching you thrive with your ADHD-have helped me tremendously.'

Emma realised she could be a lighthouse for her community and inspire many other business owners. And the more she trusted her light, gift and vision, the more her business growth accelerated.

Her business accelerated when she trusted herself and leaned into reconnecting with her light. In the first three months, her skin care brand generated over $15k in online sales. It can happen to you, too, if you fully Lean in.

This step of Leaning in also applies to Emma's life. She decided to conceive her second child. She went through a miscarriage and allowed this journey to be. She trusted her vision of giving birth to two beautiful souls; as I write those words, she is eight months pregnant with her second child.

HOW DO I LEAN IN?

Reconnection is the keyword of this step and the main action of the Lean in process. This part of the process is about bringing LIGHT into your daily awareness.

I named the path of my light journey Mission to March because saying it aloud made it feel real. I also had a vision board with my face photoshopped on the Mission to Mars movie poster. It allowed me consistency and reminded me of my purpose when challenges or doubts arose.

This reminds me of a special scene in the book *Alice in Wonderland*:

'Would you tell me, please, which way
I ought to go from here?' asked Alice. 'That
depends a good deal on where you want
to get to,' said the cat. 'I don't much care where–'
she responded. 'Then it doesn't
matter which way you go.' said the cat.

LEWIS CARROLL
Alice in Wonderland

Now is the time to declare your light. Your vision, mission, purpose and calling. Maybe it is a lifetime thing. Maybe it is a goal you aspire to right now. But this vision, this purpose, is what leads you to your light.

It could be your own business, your new offering, writing a book or the lifestyle you want to build around your business (like Samantha Wills did). This is yours. Not anyone else's.

Each time the vision might evolve, but the concept is the same. Be truly and deeply connected to yourself and what you want. You have the answers within you. That is your intuition.

It is your time, right now, to declare your vision. Journal[11] it, manifest it. Make it real by drawing, crafting a vision board, singing, or creatively bringing your vision to life in another way that feels right for you.

More of the action comes later. But right now, it is about bringing it from ether to matter, from the invisible to the visible. Your alignment, through action, will come later.

---

11 NOTE: Journaling is simply writing down your thoughts and feelings to understand them more clearly. How to journal? Set a five to ten-minute timer, open your journal and begin writing! Don't censor yourself. Don't worry about spelling or grammar. Just write one sentence after another. When you understand this work, you might try to stop negative thinking as it is presented. This is a HUGE mistake; you must let your emotions and feelings flow onto the page. Don't stop until the timer is finished, then read what you wrote. This is what you truly desire, your vision coming from your intuition.

PUTTING IT INTO PRACTICE

Listen to the meditation at www.lightitbook.com to connect with your vision.

Now try to say aloud: '*I am the Sacred CEO of [insert your vision].*'

Ask yourself: Who do I get to become for this vision to come to life? What risks have I decided not to take, and what risks have I decided to take? Take one minute to allow this vision to speak back. Let it respond to you.

Then, make a collage of everything you aspire to. Manifest it. Include everything that came to you during the connection to your vision. Think about what you want and put it into the picture: What vision are you trying to create?

Your brain is focusing on the image rather than the words. Take time to collect the images and take time to do this practice. Look at it daily to refresh your memory.

Maybe you journal about it, sing, draw, paint, or do something else creative. You are not making an action plan; you are simply declaring it.

If you create anything that represents your vision, email it to me at hello@essentialshift.co or share it on your Instagram story and tag me @essential.shift.

KEY MESSAGES

- Leaning in is about stepping up and connecting with your vision.

- Leaning in is about being, not doing.

- When you Lean in you have to trust yourself.

- When you declare what you actually want, not what people think you want, the magic starts to unfold.

4

ILLUMINATE

THE PATH BACKWARDS

Did you ever do maze puzzles as a child? I now offer these to my girls when we go to a restaurant (to keep them busy). I remember doing these as a child, but as I was a bit competitive, I always looked for the result (I may have cheated in a game or two).

I wouldn't waste my time drawing from start to finish, getting stuck and starting again. I would solve the maze backwards.

You might think, 'Doesn't that ruin the fun?' However, later in life, it made a lot of sense to me. Solving a maze puzzle is no different from wanting to achieve something in life and business. Instead of starting without guidance, it is better to have a process of moving forward.

Think about training to run a marathon. You wouldn't just get off the couch and start running. You would have a plan and milestones with the end result in mind. So you work backwards from the goal to each milestone, one at a time. That is why we go backwards in the maze. We start at the end goal and who we need to BE to achieve this outcome. From that vision, we work our way back until we understand where we need to start and what path to take.

This is exactly how you Illuminate your path forward. Thinking backwards gives us the confidence to know what we want to achieve.

Now you already have your vision. You have used the Lean in process to determine what you want. You've honoured the time to BE. Now it is time to work on the path to DO what you want. Remember in the previous chapter the step: BE—DO—HAVE.

It is about going to the final destination and working backwards to know exactly where to start.

It is your turn to Illuminate your path towards the business you have been dreaming of. Who is with me?

WHAT IS ILLUMINATE?

If you type 'Illuminate' into Google, what comes up is this perfect definition from Collins Dictionary: 'To make (something) visible or bright by shining light on it; to light up.' When you Lean in, you light up. From that light comes the illuminated path for you to move forward with your dreams and vision. But as the maze tells us, we must work backwards to go forwards (there is an exercise on this at the end of the chapter). You find this path when you declare your vision and purpose. When you take the first step. This illuminated path is waiting for you to take the next step.

You will not see the illuminated path if you don't take that first step of Leaning in. So make sure you step in and fully embrace this next vision. If you don't have a clear vision yet, it is okay. It takes time if you are not familiar with this approach. Be gentle and compassionate with yourself. You can listen again to the vision meditation and return to the exercise in Chapter Three as many times as you want. Keep reading; it might come later!

When the path is illuminated, you can take action. You come to embrace the doing phase. Please don't confuse this with hustle. I will not sit here and tell you this doesn't take work, because it does. You have to do more than set the vision and sit back and wait for it to happen. But you don't have to hustle. You are reading this book because the hustle isn't working. But when you do the work, ensure it is healed and balanced. You want to feel like this:

- Empowered
- Accountable
- Accomplished
- Confident

- Strong
- Decisive
- Reasonable

Not this:

- Fearful
- Worthless
- Angry
- Arrogant

- Reckless
- Doubtful
- Unfocused

You don't have to have it all figured out when you start the LIGHT process. The illumination is the how, the way to go, the path.

Living in alignment with your soul-calling cannot be done with compromise. You have to make big, bold and courageous moves.

The ones led by your inner light, the ones in your heart. Do you know that heart and courage are deeply connected?

Brené Brown, in her book *I Thought It Was Just Me: Women Reclaiming Power and Courage in a Culture of Shame*, explains this connection beautifully. 'Courage is a heart word. The root of the word courage is cor—the Latin word for heart. In one of its earliest forms, the word courage meant "To speak one's mind by telling all one's heart." Over time, this definition has changed, and today, we typically associate courage with heroic and brave deeds.'

Below is a beautiful representation I love sharing with my clients about the power of choosing one path.

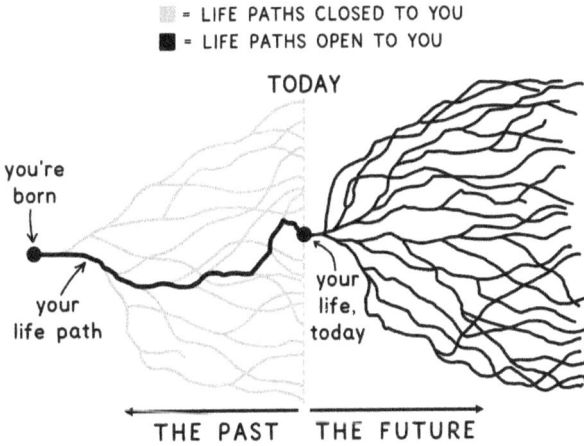

= LIFE PATHS CLOSED TO YOU
= LIFE PATHS OPEN TO YOU

TODAY

you're born

your life path

your life, today

THE PAST   THE FUTURE

Figure 4.1. Tim Urban is the author and illustrator of the blog *Wait but Why*, which is one of my favourite blogs and explores topics from AI to leadership and marriage.

You open new paths whenever you choose one that aligns with your mission and purpose. The worst thing that can happen to you is not choosing a path and staying stuck.

When the path is illuminated, it doesn't mean it will all work out from the beginning. But you must know you are being guided in the right direction.

Every mistake, challenge and failure is part of the process. They are opportunities to learn. When I was a little girl and broke a glass or a plate while emptying the dishwasher, my mother would say: 'Only those who don't do anything don't break anything.' Quickly, I learned how to empty a dishwasher without breaking anything. When you trust and honour that failure is a natural part of success, there is no wrong way. Everything is illuminated perfectly for you.

Before starting Essential Shift, I was doubtful about being a solo Founder and how to finally create a successful business after three failures. I remembered what I had learned from my previous business failures. I was always in partnerships, and at some point, I'd lose alignment with the vision of my co-founder, and we'd have to stop working together. I even wrote an article based on those learnings for *My Business Magazine*[12] entitled 'Business Partnership: The Pros and Cons'. In the end, those failures illuminated for me the path forward to become CEO of Essential Shift and solo Founder with a wonderful team around me.

---

12 https://www.mybusiness.com.au/how-we-help/be-more-efficient/ work-smarter/business-partnerships-the-pros-and-cons

So, remember that the more you achieve, the more you make mistakes. And when you make a mistake, you reflect, and the more you reflect, the more you learn—the process continues. And it is cyclical, like everything. You are building a masterpiece; finding the best path forward will take time. Your path to success sometimes involves trial and error, iteration, and small or even microscopic steps. Be patient and welcome the hiccups along the path and trust that they are happening for you, not to you.

I love this line that Cherie Conan, CEO of The Digital Picnic, wrote: 'Throughout all of the success … a business owner is whispering "f*ck," almost every step'a'the'way: it's why business ownership really isn't suited to everyone, actually.'[13]

It is a great reminder of your growth and resilience as a woman in business. And this is where I'd like to reframe Cherie's 'Oh F*ck' moment as our 'Light Bulb' moment. The moment when you reflect on the failures, and they actually Illuminate your path forward. So I created this original representation of business progress shown in Figure 4.2. The reality of the illuminated path is way more vibrant than the myth.

---

13 www.linkedin.com/in/cherie-clonan

MYTH ABOUT THE ILLUMINATED PATH:
What you think progress looks like

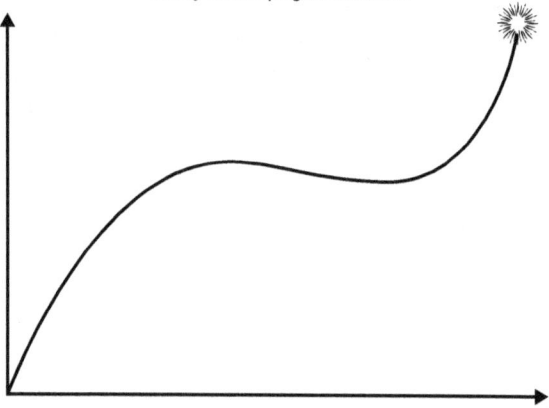

REALITY ABOUT THE ILLUMINATED PATH:
What progress actually looks like

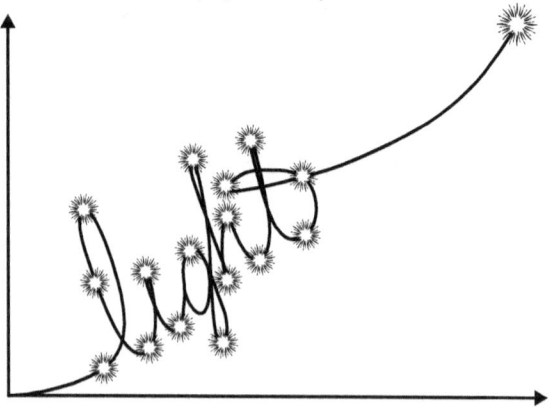

Figure 4.2. What Success Looks Like, a succession
of 'light bulb' moments by Laetitia Andrac

When was your last 'OMG' Light Bulb Moment when things made sense? I have daily moments like this; it is all about honouring them and trusting that it is taking me on the path I need to take. Remember that famous quote: 'Imperfect action is better than perfect inaction,' by Harry S. Truman. Don't let the 'stuff up' or things not going to plan stop you from starting. Why? Because there will always be a Light Bulb Moment around the corner.

Of course, there are moments of genius where you see all the paths and know which one you need to take. You tap into the intuition you trust. You go down the illuminated way, and you see what is next. Every single time, the next step is waiting for you.

So how are you going to get started?

TAP INTO YOUR
INTUITION TO ILLUMINATE

If you think about the shine of your light, think about a candle. Even better, light a candle now. Lighting a candle and watching the flames shows you a few things. It needs space to spark. Its glow will radiate and light up what is close, and even the art of watching the flame will help give clarity.

Can you see how this relates to you and your purpose, calling and passions? Giving space, allowing time, watching the 'flame' for clarity and seeing the direct path in front of you? Like the saying 'One step at a time.'

I invite you to first light a candle and see this process, to witness it. Watch the candle and soak in the energy. Be the candle, the light in your hands, to see the way forward more clearly. I want to help you feel like a winner in your business every day.

Although I have an exercise for you in this section, I want to tell you something. If you are ever presented with multiple paths, go with your intuition. I will put a practice in here to help you connect with that. You have started to do the work to tap into your intuition, and now we are about to do more.

The beautiful thing about the illumination is that no choice is wrong. You will only learn, only grow. When you trust this, every path will always be the right one for you when you choose it. But you must tap in and connect to know which one it is.

The how within Illuminate is the do. You must take the first step to know what to do next. To understand the process. Once you have, you reflect. So let me guide you through some quick exercises to help you with the Illuminate process.

Awaken your intuition

First, we must explain the difference between knowledge and education.

- Knowledge is a natural evolving process that is within everyone. Within our own potential. Within our deep connection with the universe.

- Education, which is what teachers, scientists, researchers, and so on do, is an external manifestation of information.

So, education is essential for our mental faculties and growth. Yet, it is insufficient to awaken our intuition and intuitive ability. For this, you need to connect with your inner knowing, your knowledge.

The power of intuitive education is that you do not need a Ph.D. or any other external education diploma to connect with your LIGHT. The exercises in this book and the rituals will naturally help you connect with your unique, wise, illuminated path.

Be prepared to use your intuition to Illuminate your personal and business path. I use my intuition to birth new offerings in my business, do intuitive pricing, and so on.

How to awaken your intuition

Step 1: Be kind!

Remember in that process to always be kind to yourself and those around you. As Kalil Gibran said: 'The smallest act of kindness is worth more than the greatest intention.' So when working on awakening your intuition, kindness needs to flow.

Step 2: Take a pause and make space to connect within

Imagine your life when you start with a pause. Not rushing through your day. I have a powerful rituals guide at www.lightitbook.com you may wish to download to help you with this. Or imagine taking a pause and meditating in the middle of your day. So many of us rush through everything, always on the go, feeling drained and empty. Your intuition will not awaken in that context. Harvest the space of kindness you've created in step 1 and remove the clutter in your life to find a time to pause and connect within. You can even schedule a specific time to catch up with yourself.

To illustrate this step, I love this quote from Henry David Thoreau, an American naturalist, essayist, poet and philosopher: 'It is not enough to be busy. So are the ants. The question is, what are we busy about?'

Step 3: Try this simple daily ritual

This is where I've experienced the most powerful practices and have seen the impact on my clients to awaken their intuition: meditation, breathwork (pranayama) and sound.

So, I'm suggesting one practice for you to try to witness as your mind starts to flow in harmony with your breath and sound.

It is called: *Pranava Upasana*, or meditating on 'OM'. OM is the sacred syllable the Hindu seers know to be a cosmic seed sound. By saying the sound, we use the entire vocal range from throat to lips, opening the connection with our vast inner realm where our intuition sits. It is a simple yet powerful practice to adopt before a longer meditation. You can do it at any time of the day to promote the awakening of your intuition.

The ritual of Pranava Upasana

Start with setting a timer for five or ten minutes. You can extend this practice with a thirty-minute meditation.

- Sit comfortably on the floor or a chair with your feet firmly on the ground.

- Close your eyes softly.

- Take three deep inhalations and exhalations. Then take another deep inhalation, and on your next exhalation, chant *OM*. Unleash your voice like a powerful golden light surrounding you.

- Hold the sound as long as you can and reduce it incrementally until it ends in silence.

- Repeat for five to ten minutes.

- When you've finished, stay seated with your eyes closed. Breathe, observe the deep inner silence, calm and light aura you've created. From that space, you can ask for guidance from your intuition and your inner knowledge and then write in your journal.

- Use some prompts from the next page to help you.

Reflection prompts for your business:

- What comes up if you finish this sentence: My next step to embrace my vision is ...

- What path allows me to share my knowledge and wisdom with others?

- What are the next offerings (products or services) I can create?

- How do I price these offerings?

Affirmations to help you:

- I trust my intuition.

- I align my consciousness with the Source.

- I open my imagination to see the best in myself and others.

- I am open to the wisdom within.

- I can manifest my vision.

FINDING THE NEXT STEP

The benefits are clear. If you don't take the first step, the action, you don't know. You don't know what works or will get your true desires. One saying that I love to quote is: 'One single action is worth more than a thousand thoughts.'

When I set my intention to leave my full-time job to work solely for myself, I cut back a day from my full-time job. I learned a lot in that process.

Specifically, that I could survive on a day's worth less income. And that I could really serve and impact more women. I would build Essential Shift into a profitable business that allowed me to spend time with my family, take time off without stress, and create an impact in my community.

The payoff is huge. It outweighs any failure you could ever imagine. Remember that quote, 'It isn't the goal; it is the person you become in the process of achieving that goal.' This is what Illuminate helps with. It shows you that there is a growth path, one that will teach you more than you ever knew before. It will help you step outside your comfort zone to live your desired life, to build and grow what you want.

You get more than just the outcome of what you set out for. You get the lessons, the journey. It is the journey that creates happiness, not the destination. When you enjoy the process you:

- Focus on what you are passionate about, and it gives life to your unique talents. When you love what you do, you move faster. This is where reflection is important. Check in, and if you don't love it, let it go in the way you can. This shows you what to say no to. What you can delete, delegate or make easier for yourself.

- Connect with desire. This is what you declared in Lean in. But when you create the process and take the first step, it allows you to connect more to the outcome.

- Embrace imperfections. Illuminate will show you that there are lessons to be learned. Not everything works out how you think. Not everything is perfect. But you embrace it. Because you know you cannot fail, only learn and grow.

When you hit the Illumination phase, you can step into the role you set for yourself. That Sacred CEO of your life and business. In the end, you will find much more than that. You will be gifted with lessons you never had before, connections with people you never knew existed, and opportunities you wouldn't have imagined.

All you need to do is take one step. Your path is there. You are the only one who can do it. I have seen many clients do this, but let me share the story of one who comes to mind when I think of the Illumination process in LIGHT.

FROM ZERO TO
SIX-FIGURE REVENUE

NAME: Jade Warne, Australia
BUSINESS: Photographer and IG Growth
Mentor, Founder of Instagram Growth Club

Jade Warne was a photographer, and she still is, but she is more than that now. When COVID hit hard in Australia (May 2021) and we went into a long lockdown, Jade's service-based business also went into lockdown. Her income and her purpose fell through her fingers. Her calling is to help small businesses. She did that through the power of her branding photos and the strategy she gave on social media via her Instagram platform and one-on-one strategy sessions.

All of that felt hard when she didn't know where her next lot of business would come from. So, she looked to do something different. Something purely online and something that allowed her to help more small businesses significantly (not just a one-on-one photography session). She booked a coaching call with me even when she had no cash flow because she knew she was looking for someone. After booking the call, she had some self-doubt, second-guessing herself about the investment. Still, she was ready, trusted me, and wanted to try anything to save her business. So we jumped on a strategy call on a Friday afternoon at 3 pm, and I guided her through meditation. She was clear in her vision. Then I opened a Google document and put the ideas together, which is what I love to do as a business doula for my clients. In less than sixty minutes, we figured out how to help her make some income and service her audience in the depths of lockdown.

Her path became clear. It was illuminated from working on her vision and thinking backwards from there. She took the steps she needed to by building a roadmap. She set up a PayPal link and some promotional material and promoted her new Instagram Growth Club membership. Within forty-eight hours of launching it, she got forty-eight founding members signing up. She created $600 MRR (monthly recurring revenue) for herself. She was then able to help more people online use Instagram to sell their products and services in a challenging time for small businesses.

She shared her content with a close friends list on Instagram and made it happen. She now delivers training and educational content to her members using the Instagram platform. She didn't need any systems, just PayPal and Instagram. I always encourage my clients to try with a minimum viable product first and validate the market fit.

The growth from there has been amazing. She grew her membership to over 150 people and is now tapping into the Instagram Reels space. She is doing workshops and training to help her audience. This all started from the illuminated path that came from aligning with her vision. The path to starting a membership online. The learnings developed from this space have allowed Jade to get more passive income-driven growth. This allows her more time with her family, and she still gets to do photoshoots and help her community in multiple ways. You can have the same impact and results too! Sometimes, you need the right mentor to help you see it and move forward.

Now Jade is growing her business with different income streams aligned with her vision. She feels lighter and more inspired as she now has a plan, some space and time to enjoy the life she created for herself. She became magnetic too and grew her Instagram audience from +30 k followers to +100 k, and her business revenue to more than six figures. In her CASHFEST workshop, she now empowers other business owners to make money on Instagram without hustling.

FINDING HOW TO GET THERE

Why must illumination be part of your journey? Remember, you don't get the illuminated path if you don't Lean in. If you see the illumination and feel unsure, trust it. Take the path. When the decision aligns with your vision and purpose, you can't do wrong.

To Illuminate is an important part of the process because it gives you the how. It gives you the process, not one you learn in a course or are told from a podcast, reading a book or listening to someone else. You fail fast or win big. If you don't Illuminate, you don't know what is working.

You also become agile. You break things down into smaller tasks. You evaluate performance continuously. You collaborate with others to help you and lead a project by empowering others around you to help add creativity.

Illuminating the path isn't about those BIG steps. It is the small steps that get you closer to your purpose.

It is about being agile, breaking down the steps, learning quickly, testing, trialling and measuring.

Just like I did in my journey to quitting my full-time job. I took small steps. Setting up my online presence on social media, creating a website, bringing on people to my team and creating offers to help me go full-time into my business and be in my calling. Step by step. Be present and patient. No overnight success is promised in this book.

But what is truly important and beautiful about this illumination path is that it will stick when you learn what works. It will show you what you can keep and delete in your business and relationships.

Why must you take the steps in the illumination? It helps you work through discomfort. It allows you to grow and evolve. Think of it like a sandcastle. When you Illuminate your path, you make a sandcastle. When it works, you move forward and use the sandcastle as a mould to build stronger foundations. When it doesn't, you destroy it and start again.

The first step in your path doesn't have to be doing something a long way out of your comfort zone. It could be something small. Something to warm you up. Before growing Essential Shift, I started facilitating circles on the beach with friends, coaching with friends and hosting retreats at my home because it was just part of the journey. This allowed me to learn my light, my calling. Maybe that is your first step.

You might be wondering: What if you are presented with multiple paths? How do you choose the right path? Start by setting your vision, clarifying your intent, illuminating one path, taking one step and being prepared to learn along the path. Let's now put it all together in a dynamic way. For that, I will introduce you to a tool I created, inspired by the transformation map (a strategy consulting tool), that has helped me and many of my clients in my strategy consulting career (since 2008). I call it the Illumination Map. Be open for this path to be illuminated as you start doing the work and be open to listening to your intuition (which you did in the previous exercise in this chapter). It is an iterative process. Nothing is set in stone.

PUTTING IT INTO PRACTICE
ILLUMINATION MAP

An Illumination Map (or I-Map, for short) visually represents the plan to implement your vision and what came up in the LIGHT framework's Lean in steps. It states the actions and milestones to achieve your vision. It is all about illuminating for you, visually and dynamically, the path forward. So when the moment of taking action occurs, there is no need to make a decision: you simply follow your predetermined plan.

Step 1: Prepare your I-Map Skeleton

- Watch a quick video to guide you and print an AO-sized I-Map template after downloading the digital format (www.lightitbook.com) or draw the sample template below on a large piece of paper. You will need it. You will need to customise both the timeframes and the categories to suit your specific purpose, as described below.

- Write your Current Reality in the bottom left corner. For instance, in September 2020, I was: A corporate General Manager.

- Write your vision in the top right corner. If it is too long, try to summarise it into a vision statement. For instance, mine is 'Impact one million women-preneurs by 2032.'

- Determine the length of time when this vision is to be achieved. A few weeks, a few months, a year or three years, five years, ten years, etc.

- Determine the timeframes for your I-Map. For example, if the time for achieving your vision is three years, your time frames could be broken down into 6: Q1: THIS YEAR, Q2: THIS YEAR, H2: THIS YEAR, H1: NEXT YEAR, H2: NEXT YEAR, and TWO YEARS FROM NOW. There is usually a higher volume of activities and milestones as you begin your journey because you have more clarity for the short-term steps and as mentioned before, clarity comes from experimentations. That is the purpose of the shorter periods at the beginning of your journey. NOTE: *Q1 refers to quarter one of the fiscal year. H1 refers to the first half of the year.*

- Determine the categories for your I-Map. These categories will change based on the nature of your vision. For example: if your vision is running a seven-figure business as a digital nomad in five years, it may include categories such as Process, Platform, Marketing, Team and Product Development. Choosing the right categories for your situation can be difficult. Don't worry if you change them a few times. Having draft categories in mind is helpful, and you'll start to Illuminate your path forward. NOTE: *You may want to use sticky notes to document your timeframes and categories so they can be easily changed as you progress.*

Step 2: Start filling out your I-Map
- Put each milestone by category, working backwards from your vision of what needs to happen (which actions). NOTE: *I suggest you use sticky notes again*

for the actions and milestones if you've printed them or write with a pencil to edit them in the book. This allows you to adjust it and keep it as a 'living' document.

- Watch for interdependencies between the actions, i.e., product development must be in place before a product launch. Be conscious of the magnitude of each change, i.e., which resources will be required and for which period. Be sure to include projects already in process or planned to start. You want a complete and realistic picture. Avoid unrealistic plans, especially in the short term to avoid burnout, but also leverage the power of compounding progress.

Remember: 'Most people overestimate what they can achieve in a year and underestimate what they can achieve in ten years.[14]'

Step 3: Review your I-Map regularly
- Keep your I-Map visible so you can follow up regularly to ensure that actions and milestones are achieved.

- When you review, identify what you need to achieve some of the actions: hire someone, invest in another platform, clarify your processes, to name a few.

---

14 It's unclear exactly who first made that statement, when they said it, or how it was phrased. The most probable source is Roy Amara, a Stanford computer scientist. In the 1960s, Amara told colleagues that he believed that 'we overestimate the impact of technology in the short-term and underestimate the effect in the long run.' For this reason, variations on that phrase are often known as Amara's Law. However, Bill Gates made a similar statement (possibly paraphrasing Amara), so it's also known as Gates's Law.

Need more support? Don't worry. I have created a video for you! You can access that at www.lightitbook .com.

Let me share a real example from one of my Business Birthing Retreats, in which I guide entrepreneurs through the LIGHT framework in person over three days.

Sarah had the vision to serve more service-based business owners (she is in the product business owners space). She also loved facilitating retreats, as she has done this in the past for clients who were product-based business owners. This was her vision. So within the method of Illuminate, we used the Illumination Map to work backwards (like the maze).

We set the vision, then we worked out what she would need.

These things included: the marketing stream of work (content, Facebook ads, etc.), operational stream of work (logistics), launch plan (what dates you will launch, when you will launch and how) and communication stream of work (who needed to know what). From these four elements, we worked on what line of work formed under each. So rather than working directly on organising the retreat and finding a venue, we worked on what the retreat would look like and what elements would need to be done to market and sell this retreat.

By the end of the Business Birthing Retreat, we had the retreat mapped out without any venue booked. Her plan from there was to sell this vision. Sarah eliminated the overwhelm of organising this retreat because all the core elements were created without needing a space to host. Starting by finding a place to host would have resulted in hours of internet research and going down the rabbit hole of self-doubt and procrastination. Thanks to the I-Map, now she has everything lined up agilely and can sell her idea!

Once you have the vision, you work backwards on the plan, and the path becomes illuminated. You then know what needs to be done. It is about leading from the future in the present moment. Embracing your vision in the now and aligning each step towards the vision and focusing on what's essential.

It is like building and creating a course. Many entrepreneurs have the vision for the course and create everything, but don't find anyone to buy it. Instead, I often recommend connecting with the vision and bringing that energy and passion to the present moment to start selling the course and the vision. Then once the entrepreneur has sold a few spots, they return and create the needed material. Not convinced? Yet it is the same approach as paying for your college classes before you take them, paying for a play or movie before you see it, or paying for a flight before you board the plane. This is how most products and services work in the real world yet many entrepreneurs make the mistake of creating polished offerings before selling them.

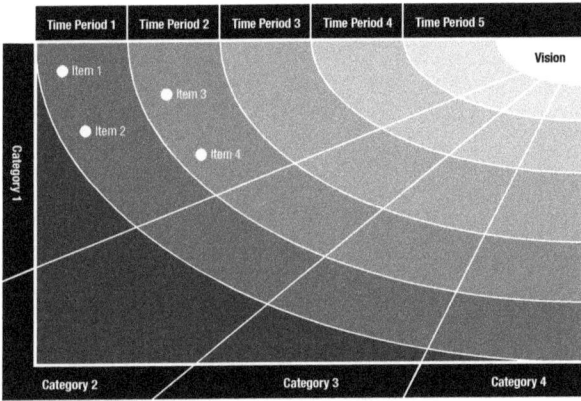

Figure 4.3. The Illumination Map by Laetitia Andrac

Start this I-Map and fill it out using your intuition. Set a timer on your phone and start. Remember, you can always edit and strengthen the plan later. You just need to get started.

KEY MESSAGES

- When you Lean in, the path forward becomes clear. This is known as Illuminate.

- To get the direction, you must work from the vision backwards.

- Some actions might not seem clear, but they will come.

- Remember, there is no wrong path forward; the wrong path is taking no path at all.

- Build your plan using your intuition, and remember, you will learn along the way.

5

GATHER

HAVE YOU HEARD the saying, 'It takes a village to raise a child?' Well, in my eyes, a business is no different. Two elements came to mind when I was thinking about the concept of 'Gather', (this next stage of the LIGHT method). What came to me was a TED Talk I watched around a study that discussed how to live a healthy and happy life. It came down to the people around the community we built.

The Harvard study showed that embracing community helps us live longer and be happier overall. When I think about building a business that makes me happy, it also means having a community—to Gather the people around me.

Through this long study (eighty years), Harvard wanted to find clues to leading healthy and happy lives.

Director of the study, Robert Waldinger, said, 'The surprising finding is that our relationships and how happy we are in our relationships have a powerful influence on our health... Taking care of your body is important, but tending to your relationships is a form of self-care too. That, I think, is the revelation.'

Waldinger recorded a TED Talk called *What Makes a Good Life? Lessons from the Longest Study on Happiness*, which has been viewed millions of times. In his studies, he found the impact loneliness had on people and discovered that it was the cause of many other issues, such as drug use and alcoholism.

So, what does this have to do with business? If a leading cause of happiness is community and connection, you'll want to build a thriving business in a community you love. The writing is on the wall.

This is why I built a community-led business with Essential Shift. It started by gathering friends in person in the circle at my place or in local venues. This was before the pandemic, but when COVID hit, like many businesses, I had no choice but to pivot online to survive.

This business was in its infancy when I pivoted online, and I didn't know if it would be the end of the business or an opportunity for growth. So, I started an online membership and facilitated online circles like I had been doing in person before the pandemic. Moving online enabled me to Gather even quicker with an aligned community of unique and diverse perspectives, life experiences and businesses.

I could connect with women in every part of the world, rather than just in Sydney, Australia. It is truly nourishing. Nurturing this unique and inclusive community with a deep sense of belonging, even online, led me to impact over 1,000 people and have my $111k month in revenue within the first eighteen months of creating Essential Shift.

There is no competition, just community. It is about developing with your community and investing in the energy of collaboration. We are all unique and have unique experiences and offers to share. Rather than trying to 'do it all', connect with community members. That type of energy is one you want to harness in business.

Think about the circle you surround yourself with in business—are they supporting you? Are they guiding you? Maybe you don't have one at all? It is time to add this to your business plan. If you want to build a business you love, one that allows you to trust yourself, it is time to build a community around you. Gather is about more than just community; this chapter will explain why.

WHAT IS GATHER?

You Gather within and with your community to find and build your unique light and path. I want to introduce the two elements of Gather—to Gather *within* (yourself) and *with* (your community).

To *Gather within* is the internal element of this concept. The Gather process is about gathering all you have. Your knowledge, feedback, and putting together something from the past to inform the future. We all start from something. You Gather what you know, and then you can build on this momentum. Momentum in physics is defined as 'mass in motion'. The amount of momentum an object (project or offering) has depends on how much it moves and how fast. Momentum depends upon the variables of mass and velocity. The momentum of an object is equal to the mass of the object, multiplied by the velocity of the object (or, in this case, project):

$$\textbf{Momentum} = \textbf{mass} \times \textbf{velocity}$$

So, think about it this way for your business:

- Mass is your knowledge, life and work experience, and

- Velocity comes from your ability to make decisions (rather than staying stuck).

It is important in this step to take stock of everything you know (mass). The speed (velocity) is what you do with that information. Remember, you don't start with nothing.

The Gathering within is asking yourself: 'Who am I, and where am I coming from?'

To Gather *with* is the external element of this concept.

Once you have gathered within, you can find your soul-aligned community. It grows with time, just like a new leader within a company. Maybe it feels like a struggle to get the people on your side, but then with the flick of the right switch, you have the people to support you. As humans we crave to belong. It is proven by many studies that belonging to a like-minded tribe will sustain your motivation in business (and life) to achieve your vision because it transforms your individual journey into a shared one. It helps you in the long run to follow through with your vision and you know it is possible because those around you are embodying that next version of yourself. That's why, for example, in my journey to become a published author, I decided to join a community of authors. Your light, your path, your illumination will help you attract your village. You need both the internal and external elements of Gather.

You can't do business alone. Even though you have the answers within you from what you have gathered, you need people around you to help your light shine brighter for both you and your community.

If we look at a disco ball, we can see that it is made up of tiny reflectors that create light. They light up the whole space. This is what Gather is all about. Bringing together all the elements of light to shine on. Your energy radiates to the world, and people are magnetised by it.

But a disco ball (business) needs to be enjoyed with others. Set it up, and invite your friends, community and clients to have fun under the disco ball.

People can't copycat your disco ball when it is unique to you.

Have you ever searched for a tutorial on creating your own disco ball? I did as the analogy of the disco ball came to me to illustrate this chapter. The videos on YouTube describe the exact process you will be guided through in this chapter. What these videos all mention is the fact that each piece of mirror, when put on a flat surface, won't give the same effect as they do when presented together as a round surface. So, when the light hits a round disco ball, it projects the light around the room, which wouldn't happen on a flat surface mirror. BE the disco ball and project your light to the world.

Figure 5.1. With and Without
a Disco Ball by Laetitia Andrac

WHY DOES GATHER MATTER?

Now you understand what it looks like to Gather (within and with others), why would you do that? What does this mean for your business?

Gather within

When you Gather internally, you hold up the mirrors of your disco ball and see the reflection. Be prepared to explore your past and connect with your ancestors. Maybe your grandparents were entrepreneurs, or perhaps something from your past can help you in your business venture today. It doesn't mean you have to know everything you have gathered now. That knowledge will continue to come.

When you Gather *within*, you are shining. The radiance from within will be there for all to see as people become attracted to your light. By being a compassionate, inspiring leader, many will benefit as they feel your warmth. Light rays reach far and wide.

This also allows you to see the roots of your tree. Think about a tree standing there in all its glory. But you don't see the roots underneath. You don't see how those roots are part of nature's ecosystem. Your knowledge and past experiences are the roots that make up the ecosystem of your business. Bring them to the surface and use this knowledge to create something unique in your business.

Gather with

You find your community when you are clear on what you seek. You attract the right people to work, help, serve and connect with you.

Be open to the people you attract: 'We need each other's light. If we dishonour others' light, we don't have any light to move by. So, remember, everything living has a light, and for every light we take, snuff out or destroy, it is one less light to guide us along our own uncertain path in the dark. Everything has a right to be. Everything has a purpose of being,' said Minmia in *Under the Quandong Tree*.

If you struggle to understand how a community can help in business, let me share what happened to me...

It was October 2022, and I was having my mid-morning work break with my husband. Suddenly, I received a photo from some of the women in The Circle Membership (my strategy and intuition-based membership for women in business).

The message and photo were sent from one of the beautiful members, Adrienne.

'Truly magical' were the words used by Adrienne. You see, some of the women from The Circle Membership decided to meet in person while doing the coastal walk in Sydney.

Adrienne talked about how generous her community was and how rich she felt in her business because of the support from women in The Circle Membership. To summarise Adrienne's words, she said, 'It is such a rich place to be. You don't need to invest in all the things. This community is so everything you need.'

The women in this community collaborate, work, and buy each other's products. It is about small businesses supporting small businesses. This membership is the first offer I launched in my business because I knew it was needed.

If you don't Gather, you don't see the reflection. You have identified what you want to Lean into (Chapter Three), Illuminate (Chapter Four) and Gather. Soon you can move forward to 'Honour' and 'Transform'.

THE MAGIC OF GATHER

When you Gather *within*, your light is going to ignite. You will collate everything you know to help you reach your goals, vision and dream business because you have the answers within you. But if you don't reflect, you won't know.

It is like creating this book. I needed to Gather all my information and resources to bring it together— over fifteen years of strategy experience blended with over thirty years of spiritual wisdom. But as I continued to create the project, I gathered information as I went. Then as the path continues to Illuminate (as you learned in the last chapter), you Gather more resources to continue! It is an iterative process.

When you Gather *with*, you attract the right people. Your light grows quicker when you have aligned people by your side. When you put thousands of candles together, they are very bright. When you have one, it will create some light, but not enough to make an impact. Also, if one light (the candle) goes out, it won't make a huge difference. When you Gather people around you, the payoff is more than you could ever hope for. It creates abundance, support and impact. When you Gather this community, the community supports you in moments of doubt and brings you more of what you need.

Gathering also expands through word of mouth as people share what they do with you. The more you Gather in your team, the easier it is to manage that team, and they back you as a leader. They are doing the promotion and the expansion, so good feedback comes. You have more support when you have more people around you (team, friends, mentors, networks). When people leave or decide not to carry on your journey, they become part of a chapter of the business, not the whole story. As I always say, some people are in your team or your life for a reason or a season.

Let me give you an example. Maybe this is you right now. Your business is starting to look like the modular homes people buy off the plan. You don't know what direction your business is going and aren't even sure who to talk to any more.

Everyone on Instagram wants to sell you something, and in the end you feel like you have to go down the path of 'If you can't beat them, join them.'

You have years of experience and knowledge in various topics you never even consider now. You consistently say, 'I don't know what I want; I just know it isn't this.' So take time to do a stocktake of what you know (see the exercise at the end of the chapter) and the people in your life.

This gives you clarity on what your business needs. You start to Gather all the information you need, and guess what? The next step in the path lights up. You see what you need to do now.

You become closer to that aligned business you have always dreamed of. The best part about it is that you don't have to feel so alone in the process because you have a community out there waiting for you. Not just a community that will buy from you, but one that will cheer you on, give you advice and support you in this entrepreneurship journey.

So now, you understand why you can't do it alone— and why would you want to?

Before you go. I want you to remember this: You are not alone in this business journey. You also aren't an imposter. You have the knowledge; you just need to use it. Stay in your lane; you might see the shiny object of 'monetisation' in another business area, but remember your business vision. Remember why you started your business and what you want from it. Not what other people say you should want. Build your disco ball in the way that works for you! From there, you can't ever fail.

GATHER IN MOTION

NAME: Julie Hill, USA
BUSINESS: Spiritual mentor

You can never truly underestimate the power of community.

Julie suffered from clinical depression for nine years. It was what we called the 'dark night of the soul'. What Julie found so powerful during her healing journey was returning to herself and who she is. By Gathering *within*, she reconnected to her rituals and meditation practices—skills she always knew she had inside her—and also rediscovered her deep connection to nature. And then she started Gathering *with*. She formed new friendships and found an aligned community. I am blessed to say my community is one of those that helped and supported Julie in her journey back to alignment.

When Julie created her business, she was reminded of why she studied all those spiritual practices. She was also reminded of just how important community was, so she formed her own.

'Now it all makes sense,' Julie said during an interview on my podcast (*The Essential Shift Podcast*). Julie is now a sacred space holder and way-shower. She uses her highly tuned intuition, empathic gifts and other tools to act as a loving mirror for women. She helps them to see who they truly are, to learn to love themselves and manifest living their lives in authentic alignment. Julie is unstoppable now that she has found her light for herself and her community.

This is the true power of Gather. Helping you in all areas to reconnect to your light, even if it doesn't relate to business. Julie used Gather to build her aligned business and find a community of women who would support this journey and whom she could serve. She is now leading a thriving business and making the impact she knew for so long that she was meant to. Through the process of Gathering *within* and *with*, she trusted again the whisper of her intuition. But Gathering *with* and *within* this journey to the LIGHT framework also needs a level of surrender to 'Honour' the process, which we will cover in the next chapter.

HOW TO GATHER

Now it is time for you to Gather. It is time to Gather *within* and Gather *with*. I have created some exercises that have helped me and my clients guide the process.

Gather within: The disco ball meditation

This meditation involves creating your own disco ball. This roughly spherical object reflects light directed at it in many directions. Be prepared to create your disco ball by Gathering all the facets within and around you. Grab a journal and pen to write down what you want to remember after the meditation.

It might help to record the following words so you can listen to them with your eyes closed, or perhaps have someone read this script to you or access the recorded version on www.lightitbook.com.

PUTTING IT INTO PRACTICE
THE DISCO BALL MEDITATION

Sit quietly, preferably with your legs crossed underneath you or on a chair with your back straight. Your arms should rest in your lap, your palms facing upwards, and your fingers resting open.

Let's start by surrounding ourselves with a ball filled with light by connecting with Mother Earth and Father Sky.

- Feel where you are touching the ground.

- And as if you are a tree, grow some roots.

- See them going down through the layers of the Earth.

- Reach for the Earth's centre.

- Wrap your roots around the golden core of the Earth.

- Draw up with your inhaled breath the yin energy from the Earth.

- See the golden and healing energy travelling up through your roots.

- Then see your whole body fill with this energy.

  Repeat this process three times.

- Now let's connect with the light of Father Sky.

- Take your awareness to the top of your head, your crown chakra.

- Smile. This opens your crown chakra.

- Send long, thin silver filaments and cords into the energy field surrounding you.

- Reach up into the heavens, connecting you to the force, to the energy that holds us all.

- Feel your connection with universal energies.

- Feel the embrace of the Upper Realm.

- Draw in the yang energy from the Sun.

- See the silvery Heavenly energy shimmering through your cords and filling your whole body.

- Breathe it into you.

  Repeat this process three times.

- Now bring your attention to your heart.

- See the healing, golden Earth energy and the silvery Sky energy swirling at your heart centre.

- From there, create a ball filled with energy and expand it from your heart and around yourself until you are inside this ball.

- Imagine that this enormous ball of energy is becoming a disco ball; take your time to collect one by one the facets that are going to make it unique.

- Take time to identify each facet and mount each small, mirrored surface of your disco ball.

- What do you spend most of your time and energy on? Identify five of those activities and put each on your disco ball as one facet.

- What do you love to do, even if it is for free? Again, identify at least five of those activities, put each on your disco ball as one facet, and keep going.

- What topic do you love reading about, researching and keeping up with the latest developments in? What topics do you find yourself lighting up about when they come up?

- What are the different skills you have gained? Be exhaustive here. Each is a new facet to add to your disco ball. For example, problem-solving, selling, innovating, meditating, creating, presenting, analysing, effective communication, planning, accounting, coding, pitching and operations management.

- What unique skills/talents do you have that come most naturally to you? Again, be exhaustive. The more facets you have on your disco ball, the more vibrant you are.

- If life was a magazine, what would inspire you the most? What would you find yourself clipping out the most? What subjects, people, things, experiences, tips and tools?

- What do others routinely seek you out for or ask your advice about?

- Whom do you love? Think of each person as a new facet to add.

- Where have you lived?

- Where have you travelled?

- And you can keep focusing on what you've created. Who have you impacted? Who have you mentored?

- The more elements you collect, the more your disco ball expands and is covered with mirroring facets. If the disco ball needs to expand in size to allow these additional facets to fit comfortably, let that happen.

- Then visualise, sense, perceive or intend that this point of light reflects all around you with your disco ball and within you inside the disco ball. The light is electric violet, alive and powerful with spiritual energy.

- Stay there for a few moments and really feel it.

- Take your time to come back up when you're ready.

- Wiggle your fingers.

- Wiggle your toes.

- Take a few deep breaths.

- When you're ready, open your eyes.

- You may wish to write what came up during the meditation in your journal. It is great to anchor it on paper.

Gather with

Take your journal and spend some time doing a thorough stocktake of who you know. Then visualise and manifest who you want in your life and/or business.

PUTTING IT IN PRACTICE
STOCKTAKE AND MANIFEST

Step 1: Stocktake of who you know

1   Set a fifteen-minute timer and start listing the answer to this question in your journal: Who do I know? List all the people you know or have known, like work colleagues, friends, relatives, mentors, etc. Do not stop until the timer goes off.

2   Then add another level, answering the following questions: How can these people play a role in your vision, and which facet will they bring to your disco ball? Can they be part of your team? Your community? Your peers? Your client? Your mentor?

3   Once you have finished, think about who you could contact NOW to progress towards your vision and make it a reality. Plan time in your calendar to take this action.

4   Maybe you don't have all the right people in your life. Maybe you are ready to Gather new people around you

for your dream team, soul-aligned community, clients or mentor. Step 2 can help you.

Step 2: Manifest who you want in your life

1 Grab a pen and paper and draw up six columns (include yourself and the people in your life currently—the first question in your stocktake).

2 Then create a heading for each column: Myself, Stocktake, Team, Clients, Community, Mentor.

3 Write in the columns 'Myself' and 'Stocktake' what you get from you/them. For example, fun, love and nurturing.

4 Once you have finished that, write in all the other columns what you want from the people who represent Gather in your life.

5 Now open your heart and be open to attract them.

Your table could look something like this:

Myself	Stocktake	Team	Clients	Community	Mentor

Are you ready to take on the magic of Gather?

KEY MESSAGES

- Gathering is about engaging what you know and who you know.

- It is time to remember all your knowledge and experience, Gather *within*.

- It is time to remember who you know, Gather *with*.

- Community is huge in business. Gather it!

6

HONOUR

TIME TO LET GO AND HONOUR

If you are French, you might know Edith Piaf, or maybe you know her for being an icon. If you don't know her, we will explore her amazing story of letting go and surrendering to achieve her vision of being a known singer.

Edith Piaf was born in 1915 into a family of poverty, who were street performers in Paris. Edith was abandoned by her mother at birth and spent some of her childhood living with her father's mother in a brothel in northern France. Then, sometime after that, with her father.

Edith was blinded by an eye infection at the age of three, and didn't recover her sight for several years. This was just the beginning of the pain and suffering she experienced. But she had the vision to be a known singer. Edith held on to her dreams despite her only singing experience being busking. She honoured her talent and trusted she would be a known figure.

'I've always wanted to sing, just as
I've always known that one day,
I would have my own niche in the
annals of song. It was a feeling I had.'

EDITH PIAF

The crazy thing about Piaf's story is that she didn't see the success she wanted until a more mature time for the industry between 1935 and 1945. This is the definition of resilience and honouring the vision.

It is apparent that Edith just knew she would be successful. She trusted and honoured that her talents would get her the recognition she wanted (and deserved).

Even her songs share her strong resilience and ability to let go and surrender. The song 'Non, Je Ne Regrette Rien' (No, I don't regret anything) describes letting go of a lifetime of emotional baggage. Something Edith did multiple times in her life, not just to heal but to help her flourish in her singing career.

We can take so much inspiration from Edith about honouring our talents and vision to never give up, but to also let go of what is holding us back. To let go of the fear of failure and do it anyway. Honour can have a lot of meanings when it comes to growing and owning a business, so let's look at how you can Honour and let go to move forward towards your vision. Just like Edith Piaf did. Are you ready to channel her energy?

WHAT DOES IT MEAN TO HONOUR?

What does it mean for you to Honour? To trust and surrender?

For me, it means letting go of every story you have ever told yourself that has stopped you and held you back.

It is also that moment you realise, 'Shit, it is happening.' You must Honour it before you get the transformation, like when planning your business idea and buying the domain for your website. Or investing in a new load of business mentoring to help you with the next level. It is that moment where you have done the work and Honour what is coming from it.

Don't forget, at this moment, you might also want to burn it all to the ground and start again. Before you do, I ask you to Honour. If you had built a new house, laid the foundation and, just as you were putting the roof on, wanted to change everything, you wouldn't knock it down and start again. You would Honour the choices. You would remember the end vision: a fully constructed house.

It's like waiting for your water to break when you're pregnant. You have to Honour this time and know it will happen. I felt like this with my Ayurveda in Business course and writing this book. These things took longer than anticipated to bring to life, but I Honoured that they would all come in good time. And I experienced incredible breakthroughs through this phase of Honouring for each.

We all know that breakthroughs are often experienced as a result of many previous actions, which create the momentum required for the transformation to happen. This pattern shows up everywhere from growth spurt, sport performance to healthy habits because it all requires patience and trust. When you feel stuck on something this is also a good time to harness Honour. Like when you can't think of the name of your next offering or don't have a podcast topic in mind when you plan to write your notes. When you aren't sure about the next step in the project you are working on in your job, Honour—it will come.

I can tell you that honouring is not easy. It is a hard stage in the journey to find your light. There is so much discomfort, because it reminds you that it is all going to happen eventually. The transformation is coming and doesn't always feel good. It feels scary and overwhelming. But that doesn't mean it isn't what you want.

The penny drops when you are a business owner, and you know it will happen. Maybe you begin to feel amazing. Then you feel, well, the opposite. Don't take it as an 'Oh, maybe this isn't what I want.' Remember, everything new is uncomfortable. Honour those feelings. Remember, there are moments of tests, moments when we question everything.

When we Honour, these feelings pass. Cry if you need to (and Honour it). Feel the feelings and decide that you deserve it anyway!

Honouring is accepting. It is knowing that not everything will go to plan. But when things go wrong that will become a chance to fail fast and move on. You stay committed to your vision; to Honour is to know that the illuminated path may shift and change along that journey.

To Honour is to remember you are so close. You can't give up or lose faith. It is like the 'three feet from gold' story in Napoleon Hill's *Think and Grow Rich*.

During the gold rush, a young man was mining for gold. After doing it for months without success, he decided to quit. Sold all his tools to another man. This man started digging and found gold after digging just three feet deep. The first miner was three feet away from striking gold before quitting.

When you Honour, you don't give up. You know it is all happening as it should. Imagine if Edith Piaf had given up after all the heartache in her life. Remember, her success came a lot later than expected.

WHY YOU SHOULD HONOUR

If you don't Honour, you don't get the transformation. I know it sounds simple, but it actually is. As business owners, entrepreneurs and leaders, we are told how important resilience is. And honouring your path and timing is part of this. Remember what you started this journey for. Maybe it was to impact thousands of women, protect endangered species from extinction, raise awareness about climate change, start a business to be with family more, or live as a digital nomad. If you don't Honour the process and trust, you won't get your gold.

It stops you from giving up too early and helps with your expectations. You know it won't happen overnight. You know the process is not time bound. So, you know that when you Honour your journey, you stay in your own lane. You don't compare yourself to others.

Honour also allows you to feel the feeling without expecting to know why you are feeling that way. Sometimes you don't know the root of your emotions, which is okay. Because when you Honour what is going on, you don't need to know it all.

We must Honour because we also reconnect with our Lean in stage of finding our light. We reconnect with the vision and trust the process of doing so. This allows us to understand, again, what we are doing. Another reason we Honour is to give ourselves a break from declaring our vision, illuminating the path forward and gathering it all. Honour is a time of deeper connection because you know 'it will happen'. You don't know exactly when or how, but your intuition confirms it is in motion in the invisible realm. Success is not yet in the material world, but is coming. You don't need to create and do something as you did previously. When you Honour, you make space to BE.

You will feel things such as:

- Compassion
- Acceptance
- Selflessness
- Enthusiasm
- Perseverance and discernment
- Kindness and gentleness
- Patience and love

Suppose you don't pause to Honour what you have done. In that case, you are not open to receiving the transformation that will help you find and reconnect with your light.

As French Poet Guillaume Apollinaire said, 'Now and then it is good to pause in our pursuit of happiness and just be happy.'

How is this different from the Lean in stage of the LIGHT process? Honour and Lean in are both about being; however, they are different. If you look at Lean in as moving forward, declaring what you want and stating your vision, Honour is about standing still. Being in the present. Mindful. It is that time when you have done all you can, and now you must wait for it to happen.

It is like birthing a new offering. Lean in is the intention that you want to birth this new offering because it will help you serve more and grow your business. Then you go and do the work to make it happen. When you Honour, you have done all the work. You have the sales page and the social media marketing; you are showing up for that offer to sell it, but you now trust. You know it will sell because you've done everything. You've crunched the data regarding the conversion rate benchmark (for example). You just don't know exactly how many clients will buy the new offering… So you trust this process and tap more than ever into your intuitive self to back yourself.

Trusting and backing yourself are also important because you will be tested. This means you will be delivered other opportunities and other choices. It is up to you to stick to the vision. I remember many tests in my journey to full-time entrepreneurship; staying true to my vision was important. Some of these tests were multiple six-figure salaries with other companies. But I held true.

One client asked me, 'How do I know if something is a test?', which I thought was a very good question. This is where your intuition comes in. When something is a test, it usually isn't what you want, and you know deep down it isn't. It might be tempting and feel like a good fit, but it isn't your vision. Accepting this test would mean settling for less than what you set in your vision. Some key attributes and elements from your Lean in vision would be unmet. That's why it is powerful to have a clear written vision (go back to Chapter Three to define your vision if you haven't yet). We face tests every single day. If you answer 'yes' to the following question, it is a test: Does it make you settle or feel small?

If you are unsure, tap into your intuition in these moments to get your answer. Is this a test? Even try the flip the coin exercise from Chapter One. This will tell you.

But to summarise Honour, make sure you enjoy this phase of growing your business, of connecting with yourself again. While it feels uncomfortable, the storm always clears, and you can enjoy how far you have come. You are close to getting what you want, what you have desired and deserve.

IT IS TIME TO CREATE CONNECTION

What happens when you truly Honour? When you surrender and trust, you reconnect with your vision. You reconnect with what is happening, and you understand the path you are being taken on. So, when things don't go 100 per cent to plan, when things change, you know what to do.

You know how to feel, and you get through it quicker. You learn that it will pass. You learn that you are divinely guided.

To illustrate the power of honouring, I'd like to share with you a time I went for a retreat to give birth to my shamanic drum (which is an ancient drum of the trans-Mediterranean culture symbolic of the feminine). Birthing a shamanic drum is a deep reconnection to your roots and ancestors, a remembrance of being a medicine woman and a healer. A very spiritual journey where you use your voice a lot to sing, drum, dance and share stories in a circle. But that morning, I lost my voice for the first time ever. I spent the whole time in the car, unable to speak, and couldn't share during the first Gathering with the other women.

At this time, I remembered being told about the physical and energetic connection between the throat and the womb when preparing to give birth to my daughters naturally. So as I was giving birth to another child, my shamanic drum, I honoured this period of silence. I trusted my intuition that it was what I needed. By embracing this void, I learned a lot about myself, my lineage and the process of birthing my drum. The connection between my womb and my throat was deeply healing. Every time I use my drum and sing with my clients in a circle or a ceremony, I remember the power of honouring what needed to be. When you Honour, you get the transformation. You get the result. But you can't get there unless you learn to Honour. This allows you to remember and reconnect with why you are doing what you are doing. Why do you want this? It is that reminder.

We are always tested by our vision. When we Honour, we understand this is just a test. We know and learn the patience to get what we want, whether that be your dream business, that book you want to write or that new offering you want to birth. When we Honour that the path is there, we stop and reshift to do the work. That is when the transformation can begin—the ultimate payoff.

When you Honour, you understand that this is an uncomfortable experience. You understand just what it means to go for what you want. The process is not easy.

It is a process of learning to trust. The harmony between the doing and the being. It is the moment when you are just about to reach the gold. It is just before you hit publish, go live, head out on stage.

You take a big deep breath and Honour the feelings of nervousness, fear and doubt. You tell yourself, 'This is all worth it.'

You learned to go through the feelings, and you are so close. You can taste it. This is a moment to keep going. To reconnect. This is what makes the journey of finding your light worthwhile.

Imagine this. You have decided to cut back on your one-on-one clients in your business because you are working too much. So, you use the LIGHT method to make the plan to build your business more sustainably. This means letting go of some one-on-one clients that take up too much of your time and birthing an online course, for instance, to serve many clients at the same time.

This moment feels overwhelming and uncomfortable. It is what you want, but it feels a bit scary. It feels like new territory. You have all of this extra time, but you feel like you may have made the wrong decision. This is the time to let go and Honour—to remember what you want. Trust that your business will flourish and will allow you more flexibility and freedom.

THE POWER OF
HONOURING TO GROW

NAME: Cathleen Daenzer, Australia
BUSINESS: Sustainable parties
organiser, CEO of Little Feet Events

Cathleen Daenzer studied to become a social worker in Germany before moving to Australia. She was looking to embrace a freedom-based lifestyle, and travel was essential. While this was all part of her purpose and passion, she also knew she wanted to start an eco-friendly business. She was super creative and wanted to combine those elements with building something fun, but she was not trusting herself and her unique power. When we met at our daughters' daycare, I shared my prior business failures with her. This gave her permission to start her business without feeling afraid. She decided to build a business creating eco-friendly parties for children. I told her, 'I'll book you!' She said recently that this was her final push to Honour her path.

A few months after starting this business, Cathleen was hustling hard. She wasn't honouring her situation (being a mother of two kids and having a partner who was working full-time). She wanted to create $5k in revenue in her business but didn't want to work so many hours to make this happen.

She was part of The Circle Membership and used the power of spirituality in her business to start honouring herself. When she booked an intensive session with me, she was looking for more flexibility while building her dream life. She was already more grounded and really started to Honour the steps she needed to move forward.

Then the pieces started falling into place; she took time for herself, built more of a team in her business, raised her prices and honoured where she was at in her business. She didn't expect to become successful overnight, but she continued to take the right steps forward. From there, everything fell into place. If she didn't see the power of honouring, the power of time and consistency, it might not have happened for her the way it did. She set the intention to do 100 parties in 2022 because she was inspired to finally Honour her path and trust herself. By mid-2022, she had achieved her goal, and she delivered 303 parties by the end of 2022. This is the power of honouring.

Now Cathleen has moved into a dream home by the ocean, has a team of ten, is growing her business for impact to six figures and works in her creative zone while doing it!

She told me a few weeks ago that she is not stressed any more and gets to spend time nourishing herself. She even decided to join me for her first retreat and experienced the LIGHT framework in person, which unlocked another level of growth for her and her business. This is the perfect example of prioritising yourself and your intuition to grow a business in alignment.

HOW YOU CAN HONOUR RIGHT NOW

It is not always about going forward. Remember the formula we mentioned earlier: BE—DO—HAVE.

There was a lot of action with Illuminate and Gather. Now it is time to BE again and reflect on what has shifted and changed. This is the perfect moment to reflect and Honour what has happened.

By honouring this, you'll harness 'Transform' even more. 'Transform' is the HAVE!

Stop pushing all the time. Start feeling discomfort and honouring what is.

This is an opportunity to reflect on how everything went since you started applying the exercises in this book and connecting more and more with your intuition. Take a moment of gratitude for the abundance you have (even if it's not that much ... yet).

I recommend setting aside thirty minutes to do this. Give yourself enough time to settle in so you don't feel rushed.

PUTTING IT INTO PRACTICE
HONOURING

Pour some sacred cacao or herbal tea in a cup, light a candle, and play peaceful music to set the mood. Clear your desk and clear your mind—bring your undivided attention. Make this moment feel inspiring and important, like a date with someone you care about.

1   Start by writing down the intuitive vision that you are Leaning in towards (Chapter One).

2   Set a ten-minute timer and write down everything you have accomplished since reading this book and connecting to your light from Leaning into your vision, illuminating your path and Gathering within and with.

3   Choose one of the most meaningful accomplishments and write down what quality in you made this possible.

4   Write down the hardest parts/challenges and key turning points.

5   Write down the gifts emerging from these challenges.

6   Write any specific behaviours or ways of being you chose to leave behind to fully Honour your upcoming transformation. You need to change the input if you don't like the output. That's how everything in this material world works.

After reflecting on all of this, write your acknowledgement statement to Honour where you are at:

I want to acknowledge myself for _____ (accomplishment).

It was my _____ (inner quality) that allowed me to achieve this.

I Honour the _____ (challenge) I face as I know that it is _____ (gift).

I let go of _____ (behaviours), and I know my _____ (inner quality) will help me in the future of my business as I go after _____ (vision or first goal).

Reconnect and Honour what we are doing at that moment and why we are doing it. Reconnect with the vision. Things might not be happening as you want them. But you stop reconnecting and taking steps to get what you want. What was your vision?

Look at your vision and reconnect. Honour how you feel.

KEY MESSAGES

- Now is the time to stop, reflect and BE.

- Honouring feels like a slow dance, but it is an important step.

- If you don't Honour, you don't get to Transform.

- Think about how you can Honour yourself and the work you have done.

7

TRANSFORM

WHEN YOU SIT BACK AND REFLECT

The feeling of 'Oh my gosh, I did it' came to me once I started full-time with my business, Essential Shift. It wasn't just going all-in with the business that helped me achieve this moment. I had more space and more time to reconnect with my light. The light I lost all those years ago when I experienced burnout rekindled. What I love about the stage of transformation, is the celebration.

An example of how I reflect on transformation is from my first day full-time in Essential Shift. I didn't launch 1,000 things at once or take on too many projects just because I could. I went to my daughters' school to help other parents facilitate a cooking activity in the morning, which was something I didn't get the chance to do when I worked in corporate. I spent the day with my girls.

Even during the first month of working full-time in my business (April 2021), I went on a holiday with my family. I eased into everything because I wasn't rushing to do the next thing. I honoured the transformation and built on my momentum. I allowed myself time to enjoy it—to bask in its glory.

Often, when we achieve a goal, a dream or a vision, we are straight on to the next thing. I wasn't ready for that. I wanted to ride the wave. Then when I got close to shore, it was time to paddle back out, ready for the next one. I was building on the confidence and momentum I had built from my vision to be a full-time business owner.

What I got out of this was more time and space with my girls. Believe it or not, I also got more sales and income.

Initially, if you had told me my lowest month in revenue would be $8k, I would have been very happy. As I write this book a little over a year after going all-in I hit $8k, my lowest revenue month (it happened only once), but my highest is $111k! Once this book is published, it will exponentially grow. I hope this inspires you to celebrate the transformation and reflect. As I've mentioned, I have over fifteen years of experience in strategy consulting and went to one of the best business schools in France. I also have over thirty years of spiritual connection and ancient wisdom that I have taken on my business journey. Growth has come from that gathering of skills, from being a finalist in the Australian Small

Business Awards to being a speaker, podcaster and published author. Mastery requires patience, then quantum leap is possible.

That is also the beauty of transformation. Things that once seemed scary or unachievable become natural—they become the regular thing. That is the power of reconnecting with your light and using the LIGHT method. The impossible becomes possible, and you don't realise it until you get to the transformation part. What felt like the best-case scenario for me became my reality. It was this process that transformed me. It changed me. It is set to change you too!

THE FINAL REBIRTH

The transformation is all about rebirth. You are a new version of yourself. You became the person you needed to be to achieve what you set out to achieve. No matter how big or small it was. This doesn't mean you put a big fat TICK next to life or the goal. It means you have made a transformation.

You have done the work. Now you are on the other side. You have seen how uncomfortable it can be, but so amazing at the same time. You have realised new things about yourself and trusted the journey. You know you can keep going. If you apply this to your life and everything you do, you will succeed.

You are now living the reality of success that you asked for. It is important to remember it might not be the full picture. But it is the milestone you need to keep going. Remember, the pathway wasn't linear, and that is okay. You are here.

Think about when you did Lean in. This is what you were Leaning into—the transformation. The journey cannot start again, but the wheel can go back around. As we know, everything is cyclical. The light you are now finding is represented by the round form. As I mentioned, this doesn't have to be a huge transformation. You have connected back to your light. With this light, you can achieve more while feeling lighter. You are on the cyclical journey, and this is where you get to gear up to start again. But before you do, you must remember this path. Reflect, celebrate.

You are at the beginning of your journey, like a butterfly. The more you Lean in and go through the whole process, the more you Transform. Remember, the butterfly comes from the cocoon and sees these beautiful wings. The next thing it wants to do is fly. Before it flies, it marvels at the beauty of the wings. This is where you are at. Marvel in those beautiful wings before you head to your next journey.

Within this stage of Transform, it is important to be present before you start to look at the future again. Enjoy what you achieved by using some of the LIGHT elements to be in this moment.

Continuing the quest of your calling, whether you are a leader, an employee or a Sacred CEO, is not an overnight thing. You hit milestones and achievements, and then it is on to the next stage. But what Transform allows you to do is look at the past and what you did. Celebrate that success, then look for more.

It is all part of this beautiful process that allows you to end the cycle of reconnecting with your light and head to the next big thing.

WHY THIS LAST STEP

Transform is just as important as the other steps because it is the last stage of reconnecting with your light, but it allows you to reflect. To learn and calibrate to what you have before heading to the next thing.

The most interesting thing about the Transform stage, even when you get to it, is that you might not be fully transformed. You might still have a distance to go before you get to what you envisioned. Reflect on what you have done (not what you haven't), so you can evolve (Transform) in this time.

It is also a time to remind yourself that we don't have blooming flowers the day after we plant seeds. When you use the time of transformation to see all that you have achieved, it shows you that no matter what, you are capable. Whether starting a business, building a new offering or making a niche shift, what you want to achieve is in your power. You can do it. When you continue to reconnect with your light, you will always be able to achieve your goals.

What makes Transform so powerful is this: You are always levelling up. You are always transforming. When you connect inward and bring your light to the surface, you will Transform continuously. What happens in this process is that everything becomes less scary. You push fear away, and your comfort zone gets bigger and bigger. That process is truly magical.

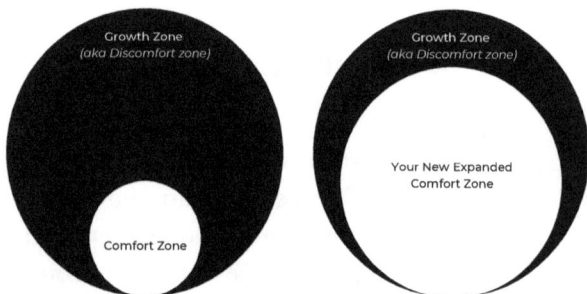

Figure 7.1. From Your Comfort Zone to
Your Expanded Comfort Zone Through the
LIGHT Framework by Laetitia Andrac

I know you see it too. I know you can spend time now reviewing everything you have achieved in the mission to reconnect with your light, and you can see the progress. That is the main purpose of this stage. Reflect. That is what I am about to invite you to do (at the end of the chapter).

Who were you when you started to connect with your light? Who are you now? This is an important question.

If you did the exercises throughout this book, this is a beautiful time to review what you did and wrote down during this journey. If you didn't do any of the exercises, no stress. I have some reflective questions for you to help with the process.

WHAT IS NEXT?

When you allow yourself to see what you have achieved, you not only see the success and the transformation, but you are also open to seeing the next part of your journey. You clearly can see what is next for you. You get to the point of what is next. You know it, you can see it.

This is when you connect and bring awareness to the realisation that you have found your light. You have reconnected through this journey and can see everything you've done up until now.

You are honouring the person you were before. You are not 'faking it until you make it.' You have made it. Now you are preparing yourself to be ready for the next transformation.

It is like that post-marathon feeling when you have proved to yourself you did it. You have crossed the finish line. You are a marathoner. You rest, recover and then decide what is next.

When you give birth to a child, you don't have another one immediately. You are present with your newborn. You are a mother. You nurture what you have.

If you look at the compound effect, the earlier you invest, the more reward you get. Say you invest $1, and you re-inject all the interest you make on that $1 into your investments. These small changes mean big results financially in the future as that money grows. The longer you do this, the more money you get. You can leverage this principle now in business and life through the LIGHT framework. It is about reaping huge rewards from a series of small choices we put back into ourselves. All big transformations come from small beginnings and seeds of vision.

Let's look at it with the LIGHT framework. Say you spend ten minutes meditating daily to plan your day with intention. Then, over a year, you see massive connection, improvement and shifts in your life. All it took was a small investment. It is about long-term effects. It is about the small things that can create big transformations over time.

You continue to Transform from this moment after the finish line. You won't see that if you don't stand still in this part of the journey. You won't see the payoff, the reward. You will continue on to the next thing without a trace. Then transformation attracts transformation.

More light will attract more light. You realise what you are capable of. This journey doesn't seem as scary. Things within this field of what you have just achieved won't feel so difficult next time. A new comfort zone is being formed and is much bigger than when you first started (as shown in the graphic on page 152).

I call you to really love this part of reconnecting with your light. It really is the easiest one. You have done the work. You have put in the effort, the time and the dedication. But you won't truly do that unless you stay in this space for a while. This doesn't mean years, months or even weeks. You know the time you need to process and enjoy this phase. Then when you are ready, it is time to go again.

All it took was reconnecting with your light. All you needed to do was hang that disco ball on the roof, plug it in and light it so it could shine. Give yourself the time to shine in this room because there are many more rooms you have to fill with your light.

Be ready. This is just the beginning.

COMING OUT OF
THE SPIRITUAL CLOSET

NAME: Ashley Roberts, USA
BUSINESS: Ritual Box Subscription,
CEO of Bloom Collective

Before we dive into the story of Transform, I want to share with you something Ashley shared with me before she spoke about her transformation. She said that when she looked up what Transform means, she found a definition describing it as, 'A stage of reconnecting and reflecting on what has been accomplished.'

Ashley comes from a family of spiritually inclined and psychic women. She has a deep history of African, Native American and Celtic spirituality. There are stories told of these women having spiritual and psychic gifts. Still, because her family was extremely conservative and religious, this was considered dangerous. It was seen as not a good thing.

As a child, Ashely always saw herself as spiritually inclined, but she kept her visions and knowings to herself. She knew it was safer that way. At the same time, she grew and expanded her skills as a varsity athlete, got a full ride to university and became an international lawyer. But her spiritual side was always hidden, and she didn't allow it to shine.

Ashley's transformation started in 2020 when the world fell apart, and everyone was looking for their anchor.

For Ashley, this was when she started to look for online communities for her own transformation. During this time, she met her first Goddess teacher. This was when she entered her Priestess training and reconnected with her gifts. These gifts were seen as a strength, not something to hide. This community celebrated her gifts. Rituals and spirituality became more integrated into Ashley's life.

The world looked like it was falling apart on the outside, but Ashely got to go inwards to build on her transformation. And one thing she learned from working as a member of my community is this, 'We have nothing to lose by showing ourselves.' This helped her journey to move forward with her gifts too.

Then in 2021, Ashley had a calling and inner knowing to start being the student and the teacher in her spiritual journey. Until then Ashley had only been working on her spiritual teachings, readings and so on with friends and loved ones. But she had a calling to share these gifts more (a nudge from her intuition).

Ashley had a burning desire to create a business that served women's radiance. To help them reconnect to womanhood and re-establish their deep connection to the cycles of nature and the moon. It became an internal mission for Ashley to help women reclaim power.

Thinking of the LIGHT process for Ashley and reconnecting with her vision, she had to go through a process of personal surrender and trust going after her vision. She really started the Lean in process when we started working together in my mastermind container, The God-dess Embodiment Sisterhood.

She did the roots and ancestry work as part of this container. She had to trust this business, which was likely based on where she was from. Working with the other women in this sisterhood helped Ashley gain the strength to surrender and trust.

Whether it is coming out of the spiritual closet or any other closet, we all have our own entrepreneurship origin story.

Ashley went on the journey of illuminating her strategy and path forward. She learned how to map out the strat-egy of her business. Then Gather came through The Circle Membership community and the Goddess Embodiment Sisterhood. She also made her own in-person community to create her space and community groups for moon rit-uals and manifestations. She gathered her own gifts and skills in this spiritual space. She went within to Gather her gifts and find who she was and what she was offering. Her Bloom Collective was birthed from this process.

She also went on a journey of accepting the work she has done. People started reaching out to collaborate with her and hear her story. Her energy was rising rapidly, along with the growth of her business and life. She has launched her Bloom Collective, a new era of stepping into her power as a student and teacher!

She is stepping into her wise woman Archetype. Ashley has turned and is ready for the next level of leadership within the community.

This is a beautiful story of Transform. Ashley went from having no offers in her business to fully stepping into her power of who she truly is. Not just the entrepreneur but the wise woman, The Bliss Queen. Ashley is ready to stand as an inspiration for all.

Ashely left me with a message that, through the LIGHT framework, we can have everything we desire: time, freedom, travel, money, love and relationships, when we step into our personal power and believe truly in the vision.

Powerful.

A TIME FOR REFLECTION

How do we Transform? Well, my love, you might have noticed that you have already transformed. You just haven't reflected. You just haven't given yourself the time to process. The Transform stage is when you need to set time aside to reflect and witness the transformation.

To help you do that, here are some journal prompts to dive into. Go make yourself your favourite drink, then sit down, grab your journal and write. See that transformation come to life. Once you have done that, you can let go. Honour the moment by letting go of it.

Eleven journal prompts to get in touch with your LIGHT and transformation:

1 What happened?

2 What changed in your life?

3 What are your biggest wins?

4 What are your hardest lessons?

5 What makes you most proud of yourself?

6 What did you discover?

7 What would you do differently?

8 What did you enjoy or appreciate?

9 What was unfolding for you at the end of this journey?

10 How has your life changed since then?

11 What is becoming possible now?

Once you have given yourself this time to reflect, let go of what you achieved. You will never forget it. Use it in your life and business. But you also want to have a ceremony to close that chapter. Even if more work is needed in other areas of this purpose or goal. Come back when you are ready for the letting go ceremony.

PUTTING IT IN PRACTICE
LETTING GO CEREMONY

This self-crafted ceremony is one of the tools we've always used as humans to mark threshold moments and let go of what no longer serves us. There's no right or wrong way to do a letting go ceremony, but here are some possible ingredients!

Create space

Set your space (with flowers, smudging, decluttering, letting the light in or making it cosy) and brew a cup of tea or sacred cacao. Make the space as you wish. Light a candle and speak your intention: to energetically complete and tie off what you have achieved and what you have worked on within this book.

Then we will use the rest of the four elements (earth, fire, air, water) to let go.

Letting go with the Earth

Use music as a 'container' for your process. Move your body, and enact your shedding. Gentle leaf-dropping, shedding. Use your voice to enhance this tenfold! Use all your body parts to enact letting go in whatever way feels right. And, after all that, perhaps take a long walk.

Letting go with fire

Write out by hand everything you are letting go of, everything you feel resentful of or outraged about, everything that makes you feel anxious or heavy, and everything that stretches you too much within this process of reconnecting with your light.

Once you feel 'emptied', burn your list with gratitude and trust, watching the ashes form, float and crumble, resting in the transformational power of fire.

Letting go with air

Take action, tidy and clear stuff out. Wash the sheets. Take the rubbish away. Take it to the next level by cleansing the house with whoever is around. Make noise, sing your favourite songs, play your drum, bring your energy into every room and have fun, shifting the juju with your will and intention!

Letting go with water

Run a ceremonial bath for yourself with Epsom salts (or regular salt) and essential oils, leaves and flower petals from your garden, and so on. Rest in the water, and imagine the salts doing what salts do, drawing out moisture and whatever you are letting go of. Allow these things to flow off you and down the drain to be held by Mother Earth.

Closing

Complete your ceremony with gratitude. Spend a few minutes in stillness, feeling the effects of your ceremony, the invisible shifts you have set in motion. Breathe deeply. Blow out your candle.

We are done. We have transformed.

KEY MESSAGES

- Even if you feel you haven't 'done the thing', you have still transformed.

- Transform is an important part of getting to where you need to be and reflecting on where you have been.

- Be present and admire your beautiful butterfly wings before you fly.

CONCLUSION

CONTINUING YOUR LIGHT

Let me leave you with another story of another time in my life when the LIGHT framework was transformational. I always come back to the LIGHT framework to help me connect with my intuition and trust in the outcome of what I am asking for in life and business. I am not an enlightened being, or a spiritual master. But the LIGHT framework was what I called on when writing and publishing this book.

Through the process of finding a publisher, I had to work on my own wound of not belonging, of being different. My wounds ranged from having ADHD and not fitting in a box to being 'too loud or too emotional for corporate.'

The LIGHT framework helped me through the process of rejection by a few traditional publishers because my book did not fit a particular genre. It isn't about business, spirituality, self-development or my life. Rather, it is a bit of all of those things. I had to continue to Lean in after each rejection, even when it brought up a lot of emotions. I knew this book would change lives, and my vision was for it to be published. The Illuminate path wasn't linear, but I followed the steps. I had to Gather my uniqueness and my community to support me. I had to surrender and Honour that my book will not belong to one genre but many genres, which makes it a unique opportunity to impact entrepreneurs. You are reading this book now, so I did Transform. I brought this book to you.

Now I am standing on that box those publishers said my book didn't fit in. I trusted my intuition, and I made it happen.

I hope this inspires you to embrace your uniqueness and stand on your box. Always Honour your light. Be aligned with your intuition, intention and what you want. Trust the path. The beautiful synchronicity of this journey is that the same day I was rejected by one publisher, another was sending a contract to my inbox.

The transformation stage of LIGHT is different every time you go through it. Like flowers, which sometimes bloom multiple times a year (like roses) while others only bloom once a year (like the beautiful jasmine in my garden).

The LIGHT framework is a process I have found and used in every area of my life. Whenever I face a new goal or challenge, I call in my LIGHT to help me create a flow to get where I need to go.

It doesn't matter what it is: relationship, parenting or any life decisions. Remember to Lean in, Illuminate, Gather, Honour and Transform, and I promise you will get to where you need to go.

You get better at applying the LIGHT framework every time you use it. The best thing about this is that you connect back to yourself. You set the vision and deeply connect with your energy to create your deepest desires.

It is beautiful. This journey is circular and cyclical. We are always a work in progress.

If you have reached the end of this book and there was an area you struggled with, go back. Go to the part of the LIGHT process you couldn't grasp. This book is your guide, your handbook. Anything you want, desire or wish to have in your business can be achieved with this process.

Carry this everywhere you go. Memorise the steps. Live fully in alignment with your heart, mind and body. All you have to do is find the light. Be the disco ball. Be the life of the party. I know you are. By now, I think you do too. Remember, if you ever feel lost, you can return to the strategies, meditations and exercises in this book to realign with your intuition and connect with your LIGHT. You can find these resources at www.lightitbook.com.

Let me leave you with this poem, from me to you:

'Be the light
Do what feels right
Be the guide
Tune in inside
I love you
Be you.'

If you want to be part of my community and work further with your intuition to build alignment in your business, head to my website, www.essentialshift.co.

With love,
Laetitia

WHAT SHOULD YOU READ NEXT?

THANK YOU so much for taking the time to read *Light It*! The steps in this book made a huge difference for me and I hope it will be transformative for you too.

If you enjoyed this book, you may like my other writing as well. I write articles regularly on my blog: www.essentialshift.co/blog

If you are looking for another book to read, I invite you to visit www.lightitbook.com and sign up. Here you'll find a list of my favourite books by other authors.

Full disclosure, I am a bookworm and I read about a book a week, so you'll get a great curated list on a wide range of topics.

Finally, please stay in touch on Instagram @essential.shift to find out about my next book project.

ACKNOWLEDGEMENTS

THIS BOOK wouldn't have been birthed without gathering around me some incredible human beings. It is not an individual achievement but a collective one. It takes a village to write and launch a book, and I'd like to take a moment to thank mine with all my heart.

To my beloved Johan for his patience and understanding for the days, evenings and solo retreats I spent writing. Thank you for trusting me as I went through this process without knowing what I was embarking on but trusting my intuition fully.

To my wild and free-spirited daughters, Zoe and Lou, who said they would read this book as soon as they knew how. It gave me strength when I was having doubts in the writing process.

To the Essential Shift Consulting Pty Ltd team, spread out in different places worldwide, you supported me through writing. Specifically, Mariah, thank you for your incredible talent and inspiration as my ideal reader avatar.

To all my clients and community, your experiences inspired this book.

To my case studies for trusting me and saying yes to have their stories be part of *Light It*.

To those who provided advice, support and feedback on the book before we hit publish.

To my Business Birthing Retreats attendees for allowing the LIGHT framework to be tested and for trusting it will help birth a new offering.

To my extended family, my guides and mentors for sharing with me all the teachings I put in this book.

To you, dear reader, I am so grateful that you picked up this book and read it cover to cover. Remember that you have a light within you. Use this book as a reminder to connect daily with it.

Send me a DM on Instagram @essential.shift and tell me what you will experiment with from this book. Remember that you don't have to fit in a box—you can stand on it to shine your bright light. Here's to a new way of being! Just *Light It*!

RESOURCES

DIGITAL RESOURCES you'll find at:
www.lightitbook.com:

- Vision meditation;
- Disco ball meditation;
- Illumination Map (I-Map);
- And more.

Tell me about your experience stepping into your LIGHT by emailing hello@essentialshift.co

ABOUT
THE AUTHOR

WITH OVER fifteen years of strategy consulting, start-up mentoring and corporate leadership experience, Laetitia Andrac has led many successful growth and innovation programs in many high-profile global organisations, including Telstra, Deloitte, Doblin, Capgemini, Bloomberg Philanthropies and the Government of France. She understands first-hand the daily juggle of successful entrepreneurs, which can leave them feeling triggered, time-poor, spread thin and burned out.

Laetitia knows these problems too well, as she experienced burnout in 2014. At the time, wrapping her head around being burned out was impossible. People like her didn't burn out. This experience taught Laetitia the importance of reconnecting with her intuition to avoid burnout. She shares this in her book, and explains her LIGHT framework. This framework has helped hundreds of entrepreneurs shift from burned out to blissed out, reconnecting them to their intuition and inner knowing.

Laetitia's business and leadership experience is backed by extensive qualifications. She holds a Master of Science in Entrepreneurship and Strategy from a top-nine business school, an International Coaching Accreditation and is an expert in reiki, ayurveda, meditation and shamanism.

Laetitia's clients value her unique way of combining intuition and strategy to find harmony and authenticity in how they grow their businesses and impact their communities. Her consulting business, Essential Shift™, is thriving and growing as she offers a unique approach to business and leadership.

She is a mother of two girls and has lived by the ocean in Australia since October 2014.